THE
CIVIL
SERVICE
OBSERVED

C.H. MURRAY

Institute of Public Administration

First published 1990
Institute of Public Administration
57-61 Lansdowne Road
Dublin, Ireland
Tel: (01) 697011 (Publications)
Fax: (01) 698644

ISBN 1-872002-35-8

Cover and title pages designed by
Gerard Butler Design
Typeset in 11/12 Bembo
by Printset & Design Limited
Printed by Betaprint International
Limited, Dublin

CONTENTS

PREFACE

This collection brings together the articles on the public service which I wrote after my retirement from the Central Bank in October 1981. With the exception of the article on central banking, their concern is with that part of the public service—the civil service—in which I served most of my working life.

Most of the articles have appeared elsewhere, and I am grateful to the editors of *Administration, Seirbhís Phoiblí,* and *Irish Business and Administrative Research* for permission to reproduce them here.

In some respects the articles have been overtaken by events, but not materially, and I have not sought to update them. I have also let stand the element of repetition which became obvious when the articles were brought together in this volume.

'It is interesting that most of the people who have something worthwhile to say about civil service reform have been both inside and outside; inside to know the trees, outside to see the wood'—Stephen Taylor, 'Radical Structure and Systems' in *Future Shape and Reform in Whitehall*, RIPA 1988.

1

The Independence of Central Banks: an Irish Perspective

This article first appeared in Administration *Vol. 30 No.1, 1982*

During the Dáil debate on the Central Bank Bill 1942, the Minister for Finance stated that:

> The government does not, however, propose to interfere with the administration of the Bank, which will be independent in the carrying out of its functions. This independence is possessed by almost every Central Bank throughout the world and is a very desirable provision (Dáil Debates Vol 86, Col. 197).

Successive ministers, governments and oppositions have acknowledged the Bank's independence. Thus on 16 April 1980, when the Dáil debated a motion relating to the increase in bank interest rates earlier that month, the Minister for Finance quoted the 1942 statement, with implicit approval. His approval was echoed by other speakers. Deputy Garret FitzGerald endorsed 'what the Minister said about the role of the Central Bank. There will be grave danger for our currency if the role of the Central Bank is undermined'. Deputy Peter Barry declared that: 'Everybody in this House on no matter what side will agree that the Central Bank should not in any way be interfered with by government or politicians. They must be independent of them'. (Dáil Debates, Vol 319, Cols. 1369, 1404) The Bank's independence has therefore not been a contentious issue, despite occasional attempts by the media to suggest the contrary.

This paper attempts to place the Bank's independence in an international setting. After some comments on general aspects of central banking independence, the paper compares the statutory provisions relating to independence in this country and elsewhere, and gives some examples of how independence has worked out in *practice*. Considerations of space have unavoidably dictated a selective treatment of this many-faceted issue; some important aspects, such as the implications of Exchequer financing for the independence of central banks, have not been discussed.

THEORIES OF CENTRAL BANK BEHAVIOUR

Practically every country, whether developed or under developed, Western or Third World, large or small, has established a monetary institution, formally separate from the machinery of government, and has entrusted to that institution responsibility for a wide variety of monetary functions. The names differ. Some of the institutions are called Central Banks, others National Banks, others Reserve Banks and still others Monetary Authorities. In all, there are about one hundred and twenty such institutions in the world. They differ considerably in many respects — in the scale of their operations, in the problems they have to tackle, in the influences they wield — but it is probable that the functions and powers that they have in common are more numerous than those in which they differ.

Most central banks are comparatively young, having been established in the last fifty years or even less. It is perhaps inevitable that many of them were modelled on their older counterparts, with appropriate modifications to take account of local circumstances. Most of these older central banks started as commercial banks, at a time when governments had limited — if indeed any — economic policies. They acquired their powers and responsibilities gradually (and sometimes reluctantly) over a long period of time. What is significant in the context of this paper is that the central bank/government relationship in their cases had not been formulated *ab initio* but rather had emerged as a consequence of the developing functions of governments and central banks.

The most important element in central bank/government relationships is the degree of independence accorded to the central bank in the formulation and implementation of monetary policy. Central banks may discharge other functions (e.g. bank licensing, control of external reserves) but these are rarely decisive in the present context. The independence of central banks must therefore be considered in terms of their freedom to formulate and implement monetary policy — that is, to determine the amount, or the cost, of money or credit.

Earlier discussions have stressed the need for central bank independence in terms of such factors as the importance of the functions entrusted to central banks, the doctrine of counter-vailing powers and the danger of monetary policy being otherwise neglected or distorted. But Acheson and Chant (1971), who have analysed central bank *behaviour* in terms of bureaucratic theories, have presented the issue in another light. This approach regards central banks, like all bureaux, as concerned with prestige and self-preservation — their choice of goals is determined by these factors — and concludes that:

> a central bank cannot be assumed automatically to pursue its goals with the same priority as society would desire. Some characteristics of goals which are relevant to the central bank as a bureau are not relevant to society's ranking of the goals.

The same authors have argued that:

> The theory of bureaucracy predicts that the central bank would not always be a neutral advocate. Its public position on issues would be consistent with widening its discretionary options . . . we are convinced that the Bank will generally not be a source of disinterested advice (Chant and Acheson, 1973).

They recognise (if only implicitly) that a bureaucratic theory of central bank behaviour may lead into a dead-end. Having considered certain 'reforms', they conclude as follows:

> In this study we have concentrated on the bureaucratic behaviour of the central bank while ignoring to a large extent the similar behaviour of other groups. Since other *(sic)* government departments are bureaus and since the legislature itself may be influenced by similar forces, the

probability of reform may be reduced and, in the light of the theory of the second best, undesirable *(op. cit.,)*.

Professor Karl Brunner takes a similarly critical view of central bank behaviour — although not for the same reasons. He argues that:

> . . . we should not expect that a monetary authority will naturally pursue the optimal social benefit achievable with cleverly designed stabilisation policies . . . (the authorities) will have incentives to trade off degrees of achievable stabilisation for political and personal benefits of various kinds (Brunner, 1981).

This is a harsh judgement; it is well to bear in mind that Brunner advanced it without substantiation as a 'crucial point' in his case against an activist monetary policy.

I refrain from comment beyond underlining the obvious conclusion that acceptance of these two viewpoints — which I reject — would heavily qualify the amount of independence which should be accorded to central banks.

Statutory provisions

Central bank/government relationships in regard to independence are in part at least governed by statutory provisions. It is interesting, therefore, to see how the provisions governing the Central Bank of Ireland compare with those relating to other comparable central banks. The limitations of this approach must, of course, be kept in mind. The political structure, the importance attached to financial stability, the institutional framework — these and other factors differ so much from one country to another that any *general* conclusions derived from the statutes must be qualified.

In the comparison that follows, I list the provisions relating to the Central Bank of Ireland, and then comment on the position elsewhere, i.e. in other 'Western' banks*.

Capital

The capital of the Bank is held by the Minister for Finance

---

*The provisions of the Central Bank Act 1989 (enacted after this article was written) do not affect what follows.

and the surplus income is payable to him.

Comment Typically, the share capital of central banks is held by or on behalf of a government minister. In the case of some of the older central banks, which evolved from private institutions (e.g. Belgium, Switzerland, Union of South Africa) some of the share capital may still be held privately but this does not mean that they are more (or less) independent than other central banks.

Governor

The Governor is appointed by the President on the advice of the government. The term of office is seven years; the Governor may be appointed for a second term. The legislation provides, in effect, that a Governor cannot be removed from office on the initiative of the government.

Comment The tenure of the Governor (and of the Board — see below) has an important bearing on independence. Most Governors are appointed by the minister/government for a fixed term, which typically ranges from five to seven years, although there are terms as low as three years and as high as eight years. In a few cases, Governors are appointed for an indefinite period, or until they reach a stated age. In about half a dozen cases, Governors are appointed on the basis that they can be dismissed at any time. Such dismissals have in fact taken place (for example in France in 1974, apparently for public criticism of government policy). It is significant that when Spain moved in 1980 to strengthen the position of its Central Bank, one of the measures taken was to provide a fixed term of office for the Governor, who previously could be dismissed at will. Appointment by the Board of the Bank does not necessarily protect a Governor from dismissal. In one country (Turkey 1978), the Minister for Finance appointed a completely new Board which then dismissed the Governor; as I mention later, the new Governor did not stay in favour for long.

As most Governors may be appointed for a second term, some significance may attach to a failure of the government or minister to renew an appointment. Typically, this failure reflects political dissatisfaction with the Governor in question.

Thus the Governor of the Bank of Israel, whose term of office expired in 1981, was not re-appointed following his public criticism of the government's economic and fiscal policy. It was generally accepted that the failure to re-appoint the Chairman of the Federal Reserve System in 1978 reflected disagreements between President and Chairman.

No such issue arose when Dr. T.K. Whitaker's term as Governor of the Central Bank of Ireland came to an end in 1976. Well before that time, he took the initiative in informing the Minister for Finance that he did not wish to seek a second term of office.

Board of Directors

The Directors (other than service Directors) are appointed by the Minister for Finance for a fixed five year period. In practice the periods are overlapping.

Comment This is more or less standard practice elsewhere, where the share capital is held by the state. The tenure may vary, however. Although all the share capital of the Reserve Bank of South Africa is held privately, the government nominates six of the twelve directors, including the Governor.

Service Directors

The Minister for Finance may appoint two service Directors (defined as persons in the permanent service of the state) and may terminate their appointment at any time. In all but four years since the Bank commenced operations in 1943, the Board has included only one service Director. With the exception of five years in the 1950s, the Secretary of the Department of Finance has been a Director of the Bank.

Comment A survey of twenty 'Western' central banks (Fair, 1979, 1980) shows that in seven cases the Board included an official appointee, although in two of these cases the appointee had not the right to vote. There is little evidence to show that the presence or absence of an official appointee is significant as far as independence is concerned. A former Governor (of a bank which has not a government official on its Board) disapproves of the practice on the grounds that 'whatever tension there may be between central banks and governments should occur outside the Court Room and not within it' (O'Brien, 1977).

General Function

The Bank's 'general function and duty' is formulated as follows in Section 6 (1) of the Central Bank Act 1942:

> . . . the Bank shall have the general function and duty of taking (within the limit of the powers for the time being vested in it by law) such steps as the Board may from time to time deem appropriate and advisable towards safeguarding the integrity of the currency and ensuring that, in what pertains to the control of credit, the constant and predominant aim shall be the welfare of the people as a whole.

Comment The second part of this 'general function and duty' is clearly based on Article 45 of the Constitution.

Most 'Western' central banks have statutory objectives or responsibilities, of which maintaining the domestic value of the currency is the most common. The statutory objectives include (sometimes in addition to the maintenance of the domestic value of the currency) some or all of the following: controlling the external value of the currency; control of credit expansion; achievement of full employment; stability of production, trade, prices and employment.

Advising the Minister for Finance

The Minister for Finance is entitled, by virtue of Section 6 (2) of the 1942 Act, to ask the Governor or Board to 'consult and advise' with him in regard to the execution and performance by the Bank of the general function and duty referred to above.

Comment While the Governor has met the Minister for Finance from time to time, the Minister's right under this subsection has, apparently, never been formally exercised. The provisions in question are a far cry from the powers of

ministerial directive to which some central banks are subject.
I return to this issue later.

Exchange Rate

The government must consult the Bank before changing the
par value of the Irish pound (Section 43 of the Central Bank
Act 1971).

Comment I am not aware of any central bank which has the
power, unilaterally, to alter the external value of the currency
of its country; this is a power reserved to government, whether
or not the Central Bank has to be consulted before a change
is made.

The Central Bank of Ireland has powers and functions (and
therefore influence) which are not discharged in all cases by
other central banks. It has vested in it the official external
reserves. It is the authority for licensing and supervising
commercial banks; there is, however, a right of appeal to the
Minister for Finance if an application for a licence is refused,
and a proposal to revoke a bank licence must receive the
approval of the Minister. In respect of licensed banks, the bank
discharges, on a non-statutory basis, the functions exercised
in relation to the rest of the economy by the Prices
Commission, the Restrictive Practices Commission and the
Director of Consumer Affairs.

Before concluding this review of the statutory provisions,
it may be useful to mention two factors relevant to central
banking independence which might be overlooked if the
discussion were confined to a study of the statutory provisions.
I refer, on the one hand, to pressures that may be exerted on
a governor to resign and, on the other hand, to the
circumstances in which a governor takes the initiative in
resigning. The dividing line between the two types of case is
not always clear and, furthermore, information in this area is
scanty and often ambiguous. We can identify cases where a
governor did not serve out his full term of office but we cannot
be sure in all cases who took the initiative. One thing is clear:
a central bank's independence can be eroded if pressure is
brought to bear — particularly if brought successfully — on
its Governor to resign, despite the security of tenure afforded
by a fixed term of office.

In 1931 the Governor of the Netherlands National Bank had to resign because of exchange losses suffered by his bank as a result of sterling's departure from the gold standard in that year. In 1957 the Governor of the Swedish Riksbank resigned at the request of the government, after having increased the rediscount rate without first consulting the government. In 1961 the Governor of the Reserve Bank of Canada resigned at the government's request, following prolonged and bitter policy differences between the Bank and the government. In India (shortly after the establishment of the Reserve Bank), in Portugal (in 1980), and in Turkey (in 1981) the resignations of the Central Bank Governors apparently resulted from tensions between Bank and government. In 1981 the President and Vice President of the Central Bank of Argentina resigned immediately prior to a devaluation of the currency which had been preceded by heavy intervention to support the currency. In the same year, the Governor of the Bank of Greece resigned following a change of government.

Some resignations were clearly voluntary, in protest at some action by the government. The first Governor of the Reserve Bank of New Zealand resigned in 1939 in protest, inter alia, against legislation enacted in that year which gave the government power to issue directives to the Bank. In 1948 the Governor of the Swedish Riksbank resigned in protest at the government's policy of pegging long-term interest rates at what he considered too low a level.

The only instance of the resignation of a Central Bank Governor in this country is that of Dr Joseph Brennan in March 1953, some four years before the end of his second term of office.[1] His letter of resignation, addressed to the Taoiseach, is vague, terse and intriguing.

> Following conversations which I have had with the Minister for Finance on various occasions during the past year and with yourself not long ago, I now consider that I ought to retire from my post as Governor of the Central Bank. I shall be glad therefore if you will submit my resignation to the President and the Government for their acceptance. I should like it to take effect from an early date suitable to the convenience of all concerned (Moynihan, 1975).

The circumstances leading to the resignation are outlined briefly in Dr Moynihan's book:

> During a period of over twelve months the Bank had suffered relentless criticism from political and other quarters and had received no more than qualified support from the Government. Mr Brennan personally had been in an extremely difficult position. When Mr Frank Aiken was leaving office as Minister for Finance in February 1948 he thanked Mr Brennan for the 'kindness and co-operation' he had received from him; and there can be little doubt that Mr Sean MacEntee (again Minister for Finance from 1951 to 1954) felt a great deal of sympathy with the former Governor's views.
>
> Nevertheless, the situation had been such that in September 1952, six months before his actual resignation took place, Mr Brennan had decided to resign on the grounds that the views of the Central Bank on matters of monetary policy had for a considerable time past been generally unacceptable to the Government and that his position as Governor was no longer tenable. He wrote a letter to this effect which he requested Mr. McElligott to convey to the Minister for Finance; but Mr. McElligott returned the letter, undelivered, and for the time being Mr Brennan yielded to his colleague's pressure and remained in office.

There was not, however, any public controversy — or even, indeed, speculation — about the resignation, despite the fact that the Bank's views on economic policy had, as Dr Moynihan said, been the subject of 'relentless criticism' in the years preceding the resignation. The official press statement about the resignation was laconic and uninformative.

Responsibility for monetary policy

This comparision of the statutory provisions governing the Central Bank of Ireland and those governing the typical 'Western' style central bank suggests that, insofar as central banking independence is concerned, the Irish provisions are broadly comparable with those obtaining elsewhere. This conclusion is subject to an important qualification; it does not take account of the provision, already mentioned, in some legislation which empowers a minister or the government to issue directives to the central bank; I return to this issue later.

However, while statutory provisions are important, they do not yield an unambiguous answer to the question of the degree of independence possessed by a central bank. This is partly because custom, precedent and practice can modify what is provided by statute; partly because there are so many nuances involved that the issue is hardly susceptible to precise statutory formulation; partly — and probably mainly — because the legislation rarely relates monetary policy to overall economic policy and, therefore, provides an incomplete description of the central bank/government relationship.

On this last crucial point it is probably true that many central bankers would assent to the following proposition:

> The government is responsible for national economic policy. Monetary policy is one element in national economic policy and, therefore, has to be integrated with that policy. The central bank is immediately responsible for monetary policy but the government has ultimate responsibility for that policy, as it has for national economic policy.

As will be seen later, this statement is close to that made by the then Minister for Finance when the Central Bank Bill 1971 was debated in Dáil Éireann. It is a proposition which, while not formulated in these precise terms by any one central banker, is in broad accord with statements made by a number of central bankers. For example, Dr. Zijlstra, former President of the Central Bank of the Netherlands, has declared that 'the central bank should be independent, but it should remain part and parcel of parliamentary democracy ... It is clear that what is at stake is indeed the degree of independence of central banks' (Zijlstra, 1979). This issue was put succinctly almost fifty years ago by a Canadian Minister for Finance who said that monetary policy involved the exercise of sovereign power and declared bluntly that there could not be two sovereigns in any one country (Mittra, 1979).

There are, of course, exceptions to the central bank/government relationship expressed in this statement. In at least two cases — Switzerland and Austria — the relevant legislation specifically prohibits the central bank from supporting any government policy that might endanger the stability of the currency, while the Bundesbank's duty to support the general economic policy of the government is subject to the important proviso that any such support must be consistent with the Bank's function of safeguarding the currency. It is, however significant that the Governor of the National Bank of Switzerland (recognised as one of the most independent banks in the world) has acknowledged that there are limits to his independence and has stressed that central banks cannot operate in a political vacuum — that their long term targets and the means available to attaining these targets are decided in a political framework.[2]

An American statement of the relationship puts the Federal Reserve System as independent within the structure of government, though not independent of government. A former Chairman of the Federal Reserve System has acknowledged that:

> In pure theory, it would be possible for the Federal Reserve, through its monetary policy, to nullify completely what the legislature does. But, in practice, central banks, being a part of the government, having a certain responsibility, and not wanting to nullify the will of the legislature or to produce shocks in the economy, accommodate what the legislature does.[3]

A study of the history of the Federal Reserve System has put the issue more bluntly: 'a chairman of the Federal Reserve Bank who ignores the wishes of the President does so at his peril' (Weintraub, 1978, 341–362).

As I have already mentioned, the statutes governing some central banks provide explicitly for a ministerial or governmental directive requiring the Bank to implement the monetary policy indicated in the directive. In most of these cases the statutes provide for consultation with the central bank before directives are issued. In three cases there is in effect a right of appeal from a ministerial directive to the government, and the legislation provides explicitly that the exercise of the directive must be publicised, thus making it clear that the monetary policy being pursued is that of the government, not of the central bank. The number of central banks potentially subject to such directives is certainly not insignificant. Among 'Western' countries the number involved is about ten; in the case of Third World countries the number would probably be greater (Fair, *op. cit.,*). Despite these numbers I am not aware of any case where the power to direct has been exercised. As one commentator put it over twenty-five years ago:

> If (these statutory powers) have to be resorted to in any large way, they would have indicated a state of tension and a lack of cohesion that would have called for even more drastic action than the issue of a directive. Either there is a firm measure of agreement, in which case the directive or mandate ceases to be of practical importance; or there is a wide measure of disagreement, in which case the directive simply becomes an additional source of trouble.[4]

While evidence is scarce, I have the general impression that the existence of the statutory power has not weakened the central banks concerned. Indeed in some cases, it has made for close, effective working relations with Ministers of Finance — or at least has compelled the two parties to avoid conflicts (Zijlstra, *op. cit.*).

The Central Bank Act 1971 extended the functions of the Central Bank of Ireland and increased its powers in regard to the implementation of monetary policy. Having regard to these extended powers, the then Minister for Finance included in his Second Reading Speech in the Dáil a statement of the position of the Bank in the context of the relationship between monetary policy and national economic policy. On that occasion the Minister said:

> There can be no question about the responsibility of the duly elected Government for national economic policy of which monetary policy is an important and integral part. The need for integrating monetary policy with general economic policy and the ultimate authority of the government in regard to both are evident. They are fully recognised here and throughout the world.

The Minister went on to refer to the desirability of having

a special institution, differing in constitution from, and enjoying more independence than, a Government Department, charged with the immediate responsibility for monetary policy ... Everywhere, subject to this ultimate need for reconciliation of monetary with general economic policy, the maximum independence and discretion is assured to Central Banks.[5]

The Minister's statement is a more or less standard expression of the role and independence of central banks generally. It might be noted that, in common with many other such statements, it is silent on the precise *operational* meaning to be attached to the Bank's *immediate* responsibility for monetary policy and also on the method by which monetary policy might 'ultimately' be reconciled with general economic policy, should the need for reconciliation arise. It is not possible to call on experience since 1971 in answering these questions, as the government has not exercised the 'ultimate authority' referred to in the 1971 statement.

Policy conflicts

Both central bank and government would regard as desirable the achievement of maximum sustainable output and employment, with reasonable stability in prices and a sustainable external position. Conflict between monetary policy and general economic policy is, therefore, unlikely to arise because of any basic disagreement about objectives. On the other hand, disagreements may and do arise about the *priority* which should be given to any particular objective at any particular point of time. Governments tend, for example, to place emphasis in the short-term on the reduction of unemployment, and central banks tend to be concerned about the medium-term dangers of attempting to pursue expansionary policies without due regard to the effects on prices and external deficits. It is this possibility of disagreement over policy *here* and *now*, rather than over policy in the more distant future, which lies at the heart of the issue of the independence — or the dependence — of central banks.

Where disagreements arise, central banks are faced with a dilemma, particularly in regard to their primary responsibility of maintaining the value of the currency and of controlling inflation. Ireland's experience is not untypical in this respect. As a small, open, economy, Ireland's rate of inflation is particularly subject to external influences i.e. to the pace of external inflation, as modified or aggravated by the exchange rate for the Irish pound. But it would be defeatist to conclude that we are powerless to influence our rate of inflation, and wrong to assume that we cannot make it worse.

The two major domestic influences on inflation in Ireland are fiscal policy and domestic costs — both of which have, for many years now, aggravated external inflationary pressures. Should the Central Bank have attempted to offset these domestic influences? Were it to have done so, in a situation where fiscal policy was not part of the solution but rather part of the problem, it would have assumed not alone immediate, but also ultimate, responsibility for monetary policy. More specifically, in a situation where domestic credit expansion was dominated by the public sector, corrective action by the Bank would have involved minimal, if not negative, credit for the private sector, and would have thrown the whole burden of adjustment on that sector. The Bank has considered that such a result would have been unjustified and inappropriate, and perforce had to content itself with ensuring that private sector credit did not aggravate the underlying inflationary pressures. In addition, the Bank has made public its views regarding the dilemma in which monetary policy was placed, the causes of this dilemma and the ways in which it should be resolved. The freedom to make public its views is an important and valuable attribute of independence and one which the Central Bank has availed itself of for many decades.

CONCLUSION

Given the close connection between monetary policy and national economic policy, there must be cooperation between

the institutions primarily responsible for each. For a forceful
expression of this viewpoint, I turn to a statement of a former
German Minister of Finance.

> It is true that the Bundesbank and the Government form
> their opinions independently. This is their autonomy and
> it must continue so. They are, however, obliged to
> cooperate, not only by law but also as a logical outcome
> of economic facts. They cannot take effective and
> meaningful action independently and without considering
> each other's position. The Federal Government cannot start
> to implement expansionary measures if the Bundesbank
> keeps the monetary reins too tight; conversely, the
> Bundesbank cannot effectively pursue a stabilisation policy
> if the public authorities do not exercise discipline. The
> independence of the Bundesbank and the government is
> manifest in their optimum cooperation. This cooperation
> takes place not in spite of, but because of the Bundesbank's
> autonomy — an autonomy which must continue.[6]

While independence can be conferred in varying degrees by
legislation, it cannot be maintained by legislation alone; it has
to be earned. It can be earned by strength of personality. It
can be buttressed by the excellence of the work done by the
bank — a point well expressed by Louis Rasminsky when
Governor of the Reserve Bank of Canada:

> In the final analysis, the influence of the central bank on
> economic policy depends on the respect it can command
> for the objectivity and cogency of its views as judged in
> the light of experience and on the proven degree of
> confidence it displays in performing its own specialised role.
> It depends too on the contribution that it is able to make
> to the public understanding of economic and financial issues
> in analysing, in understandable terms, the complex forces
> operating at all times on the economy and in elucidating
> the basic rationale underlying the policies it has
> followed.[7]

A decade or more ago, a German Minister of Finance — Karl
Schiller — summarised his government's relationship with the

Bundesbank as follows: 'As much freedom as possible, as little control as necessary'.

This is hardly a precise blueprint for government/central bank relationships but it is an admirably brief statement of the spirit which should prevail in this relationship. Any elaboration would merely be a gloss on this formulation.

2

A Working and Changeable Instrument

This article first appeared in Administration *Vol. 30 No. 4, 1982*

I doubt whether many civil servants would agree today with Bagehot that they 'tend to see their organisation as a grand and achieved result, not a working and changeable instrument'. If any were inclined to take this view, they would soon be disabused by the volume of public complaint and criticism of the civil service. The public might, however, be excused for not being aware of the view which civil servants form of their organisation, since few of them have made their views public — apart, that is, from the representatives of public service associations. The general silence on this subject is in keeping with the civil service tradition of discretion and anonymity. But this tradition does not act as a bar on retired civil servants from speaking their mind.

This paper is intended, therefore, as a contribution to the debate on the civil service — not indeed a structured contribution, nor the expression of an 'internal reflective urge', to use Tom Barrington's expression, but more a collection of random thoughts. Two points should be stressed at the outset. The author represents no one but himself; the paper is a personal contribution, based on some forty years' experience in the civil service and (I hope) with the benefit of six years' post-service detachment. Secondly, the paper is highly selective. It omits, for example, a discussion of civil service efficiency/inefficiency, not because I consider this issue unimportant but rather because it cannot usefully be discussed at the level of generality dictated by the nature of this paper.[8] Another important issue which is omitted is the role of the civil service in regard to economic development — omitted because I have written enough on economic issues!

An ex-civil servant, writing about the institution in which he spent most of his working life, has to guard against complacency, against protesting too much. He also has to be on guard against the other extreme — of seeing only warts on the face of the civil service. It is no consolation to know that someone who steers a middle course is often accused by both extremes. But I start with one advantage; I know from years of experience at international meetings that Irish civil servants do not suffer in comparison with their counterparts abroad. This may be regarded as faint praise; it certainly is no argument against change. Since the need for change is a recurring theme in this paper, let me emphasise at the outset my conviction that the civil service has contributed to the establishment and consolidation of parliamentary democracy in this country, has served the State well, and can serve it better in the future. With Othello, the Irish civil servant can claim that 'I have done the state some service'. It is less certain that he can, with Othello, add 'and they know't'.

THE DEVLIN RECOMMENDATIONS

By Devlin I mean, of course, the Report of the Public Services Organisation Review Group. It is clear in retrospect that Devlin's terms of reference were too wide and that, as a result, the Devlin Report covered too wide an area. I have specifically in mind that part of the Report in which the Group recommended the 'ideal' division of public sector work among Departments of State, including the creation of some new departments and the suppression of some existing ones. These recommendations did not command universal assent — hardly surprising since, in at least some cases (including, to my certain knowledge, the Department of Finance), they had not been grounded on discussions with the Departments concerned. Moreover the significant Departmental changes since 1969, including the sixfold increase in the Department of the

Taoiseach, showed scant regard for the Devlin recommendations, and this contributed to the diminishing esteem in which
the Report was held; the establishment of the Department of
the Public Service was, indeed, the only major institutional
change which followed a Devlin recommendation and even
in this case the Devlin recommendation that this portfolio
should be held by the Minister for Finance, while initially
followed, was later discarded.

My main objection to the Group's wide terms of reference
rests not on these particular issues but rather on the fact that
the central and decisive message of the Report was thereby
obscured and weakened. That message was, of course, the
imperative need to ensure that Ministers and senior civil
servants had ample time to devote to policy formulation and
review, and that, towards this end, they should disentangle
themselves from excessive preoccupation with policy
execution. The creation of Aireachts and executive offices was
seen as the means to this desirable end.

There was, of course, nothing new about this line of
thought. As long ago as 1953 Professor Patrick Lynch had
written about the public service that: 'Its higher officers must
not permit themselves to become over-burdened with work,
so harassed by pressure and preoccupied by action that they
have too little time for serious thought' (Lynch, 1953); a senti-
ment which was echoed on the same occasion by Professor
John O'Donovan who saw the over-burdening of the higher
civil service as 'by far the greatest danger to which the public
interest here is exposed at present in relation to the civil service'
(O'Donovan, 1953). Some years later Dr T.K. Whitaker spoke
in similar terms:

> I am not sure now if the biggest problem after all will not
> be one of organisation — how secretaries and other senior
> officers can organise their time and work so as to get away
> from their desks and the harassing experiences of everyday
> sufficiently to read, consider and consult with others in
> order to be able to give sound and comprehensive advice
> on future development policy (Whitaker, 1961).

I suggest that there would now be little disagreement with the

central message in the Devlin Report, although not all would
accept the remedy proposed in it. Why then has so little
effectively been done about it — thirteen years after that Report,
and nine years after the establishment of the Department of
the Public Service? There is no simple, unique answer to this
question. If however I had to settle for one answer, I would
single out the lack of commitment to reform by politicians and
by the civil service.[9] I discuss the role of the civil service
later; here I address myself to that of the politician.

Many commentators have stressed that political
commitment is essential if major changes are to be effected in
the civil service. They have emphasised that this commitment
is particularly important if the Aireacht concept is to be
successfully introduced, since it significantly affects Ministers'
responsibilities and influence. The Public Services Advisory
Council has repeatedly drawn attention to this requirement.
One can read between the lines of their reports that they
consider that this political commitment has been lacking. I
suggest that the Council might serve the cause of public sector
reform better if they bluntly laid the blame — or at least a major
part of the blame — where it rests.

A discussion of why this political commitment was not
forthcoming lies outside the scope of this paper and indeed
beyond the ken of its author. I suspect however that the
explanation lies as much in a failure to grasp the importance
of the issue as in an unwillingness to loosen the grip on the
reins of power and influence. The lack of commitment had a
number of causes: a general disinterest in the subject, lack of
pressure from the civil service, a reluctance to put political
careers at risk in espousing such a long-term, obscure and
difficult cause, the increasing pressure of other work, most of
which seemed more important and more urgent than public
service reform.[10] Whatever the reasons, this lack of political
commitment was hardly an inspiration for the civil service.
While I would not, on that account, absolve the service from
its responsibilities, I can readily understand the widespread
feeling of cynicism which was engendered by the lip service
paid by politicians to reform.

I discuss later the role of the civil service in relation to the
reform of the civil service and why that role has been so

inadequate. Here I am concerned with one admittedly crucial aspect of reform, namely the Aireacht concept. Even accepting that this could not be introduced without ministerial acceptance (and of course legislative authority), the civil service can hardly wash their hands of blame. At the very least, they (or rather we, since for much of the period I was one of their company) had a responsibility to push matters to the limit and, if we judged that worthwhile progress was unlikely, to devise and press for alternative remedies. It might well be objected that my judgment of progress on the Aireacht front is too harsh, that significant advances have been made and that the concept is alive and well developed — in other words, that I am overlooking the fact that the concept has been introduced on a trial, *de facto* basis in most Departments.

To argue on these lines runs the risk of confusing shadow with substance, of form with content. Even allowing for the fact that the experiments to date lack the legislative basis required to underpin the Aireacht concept, there is little evidence to suggest that they have made any significant difference, have gone any noticeable distance towards achieving what the Devlin Group and others before them had in mind. I may, of course, be wrong on this but I am not aware of any published research on the difference, if any, which these experiments have achieved. What significance should be attached to the fact that in a recent formulation of its objectives the Department of the Public Service has placed the advancement of the Aireacht concept fairly low in the list?[11] It would hardly be surprising if the Department were having second thoughts about the primacy to be attached to what has turned out to be such an elusive concept! It has had to soldier on against political indifference and without any real cooperation from its colleagues.[12] It does not need to be reminded that 'it is all too beguiling an error to suppose that some institutional trick can be an adequate substitute for the right policy decision' (Brittan, 1969) — and, I would add, the commitment to carry through the policy decision.

I submit that it is time to have a hard look at the Aireacht concept, to decide either to abandon it or to take immediate steps to ensure that it will be implemented in full within a few years. There are, of course, some who have argued that the concept is faulty, that the separation of policy and execution is either undesirable or unworkable, or both. I don't agree, but surely we are now in a position to *test* this proposition. It might also be argued that, even if the test were negative, the Aireacht concept does not yield results commensurate with the trouble involved — not least of which is the fundamental political changes involved. Again, it should by now be possible to form some view on the truth or falseness of this viewpoint. The cause of civil service reform is, in my opinion, harmed by continuing to pay lip service to a concept which, however sound and valid in principle, has not proved to be operational. But before we reject the Aireacht concept we must consider whether there are any other methods of achieving the objective which the Devlin Group had in mind — namely, reducing the myriad demands on the time of Ministers and senior civil servants so that they might have adequate time for policy formulation and review. The fact that the Devlin prescription may have to be abandoned does not invalidate the Devlin diagnosis.

The Devlin recommendations covered a much wider area than the Aireacht concept but I have concentrated on this aspect because it is important in itself and also because so many of the other Devlin recommendations turn on it. I must be careful to avoid conveying the impression that the lack, or slow pace, of administrative reform in the past ten years can be laid at the door of the specific recommendations proposed by Devlin. Given the lack of political and administrative commitment to change, it is likely that the same fate would have befallen any alternative set of recommendations. It might, however, have helped, as I have already mentioned, if the Devlin Group had confined their recommendations to the Aireacht concept and immediately related issues. This might have concentrated minds wonderfully.

It may well be that the difficulties in the way of administrative reform have been underestimated. The fundamental task 'is to integrate the authority which comes from a popular election with that which derives from professional knowledge and experience, while upholding the principle of ultimate political control' (R.J.K. Chapman, 1978), a task which grows in complexity and difficulty according as the public sector is expanded. Responsibility for administrative reform cannot be left *entirely* in the hands of the administrators (*quis custodiet ipsos custodes?*) and cannot, by definition, be entrusted solely to politicians. How to achieve a proper balance and effective working relationship between these two groups lies at the heart of the problem. Looked at from another aspect, the problem appears as one of how to engage the commitment of a government machine that is both the agent and the object of change (Kellner and Crowther-Hunt, 1980, 286). These are issues in which Parliament might be expected to play a decisive role, in which back-benchers might effectively flex their political muscles, in which annual debate on the reports of the Public Service Advisory Council might serve as a catalyst of change ... But a Parliament which has been so remiss in reforming its own procedures is hardly likely to be active, or if active, effective in the cause of administrative reform.

I referred earlier to the lack of civil service commitment to reform. Some of what I have to say later will, I hope, substantiate this statement. One reason why commitment is less than full is the fragmented nature of the civil service — a feature to which Northcote and Trevelyan drew attention some one hundred and thirty years ago. *Plus ça change...!* In one sense there are as many civil services as there are Departments of State. The unity of the civil service in terms of common standards and procedures (recruitment, pay, promotion, discipline etc.) has to be offset against the federal qualities which stem from the automony of each Department. It is true that there was (and maybe still is) a head of the civil service but this was an informal title. The holder was hardly even *primus inter pares*, and certainly was without any power to command.

The Devlin Report was aware of the divisive nature of the civil service but rather surprisingly concluded that not alone was it a seamless garment but also that, together with local authorities and state bodies, it constituted a 'single' public service; one might remark, in passing, that the only sign of unity which the public service shows are the attacks which the members of the family make on each other. Certainly, as far as the civil service is concerned, there is no evidence of cohesiveness on the subject of civil service reform. Can it be doubted that this is a hindrance to the development of a commitment to such reform? Few civil servants accepted an individual responsibility for reform, and the service as a whole did not accept a collective responsibility. It is difficult to resist the comment that there was a 'professional predilection' for the *status quo*. A civil service which regarded itself as a profession (a subject to which I turn later) would have regarded the reform of the service as an obligation or at least would have demonstrated that reform was not necessary, if such was its conviction. To some extent, indeed, the establishment of the Department of the Public Service, by institutionalising the movement towards reform, may have been seen by some civil servants as absolving them from responsibility for change; but it would be wrong to deduce from this that it was a mistake to establish the new Department.

I am not, of course, arguing that the lack of civil service commitment to reform is pervasive. There are many and honourable exceptions. It would be ungracious not to recall that the initiative for the Devlin enquiry came from the civil service (specifically from the senior staff in the Department of Finance). But if one takes membership of the Institute of Public Administration as a proxy — indeed a rather weak one — for a commitment to reform, then the record is disquieting. Leaving aside those studying for the Institute's diplomas (for whom membership is compulsory) there are only about 150 civil service members of the Institute, i.e. about 3 per cent of the total numbers in the administrative and executive grades — not that it can be taken that all members come from those grades. It would, I suggest, be salutary to carry the analysis further and to show the numbers in each of the main grades (secretary, assistant secretary, principal officer etc.) who are Institute members.

MINISTERIAL RESPONSIBILITY

Any attempt to apply general organisational and personnel theory to the civil service has to take account of one important difference between the civil service and other institutions. I refer to the relations between Ministers and senior civil servants (in particular the official heads of Departments), a relationship which is quite different from that between chairman and managing director in private sector companies. While it is easier to recognise this relationship than to define it, it is surprising that the Devlin Report did not discuss this important issue. Perhaps not so surprising after all, since in Ireland this is truly *terra incognita*. We lack the political memoirs which might throw some light on the relationship; we have no counterpart to the waspish comments of Barbara Castle and the late Dick Crossman. Indeed the lack of *published* Irish political memoirs is notable; perhaps ministerial papers in various archives (e.g. Mulcahy, McGilligan) may in time fill part of the gap. Meanwhile it may be relevant to record what a former Tanaiste and Minister for Finance (George Colley TD) had to say, in the foreword to Ronan Fanning's *The Irish Department of Finance 1922-58* (Institute of Public Administration 1978):

> As a politician, it is probably inevitable that I should notice that the book has less of the political, as distinct from the financial and administrative, considerations that influence Ministers and Governments. This is understandable in a history based on departmental sources. It is, I suppose, a reflection of the fact that politicians are not required to commit their thoughts to paper to the same degree as civil servants.

The uniqueness, in terms of organisational theory, of the relationship between Minister and secretary (and other senior departmental officials) reflects, and is largely due to, the anomaly that the Minister is legally head of the Department but is not a full-time executive, whereas the full-time executive is not legally responsible for the actions or omissions of the Department. There is the added fact that 'Government ... tends to be a relationship between a Minister who probably has limited experience outside politics and the civil service, which has little direct experience outside the public sector' (Dell, 1979). It is not surprising, in view of these factors, that the working relationships between Minister and secretary are not only unique but hard to define — indeed are variable since they depend so much on personalities: 'The balance of ability can often in the end determine the balance of power' (Kellner and

Crowther-Hunt, *op. cit.,* 238). Sampson has used the terms 'owl and eagle' in describing secretaries and Ministers; but sometimes the labels may get mixed up!

The civil servant's function — or main concern — has often been described in terms of 'protecting his Minister'. I find this terminology puzzling and indeed slightly demeaning, demeaning both for civil servant and Minister. In so far as the phrase has any meaning, it derives from the concept of the responsibility of the Minister for all the actions and omissions of the Department. This responsibility stems from the convention that everything done by the Department is done in the Minister's name, indeed is legally done *by* the Minister. As the Devlin Report recognised, this convention is a legal fiction. Like many legal fictions, this particular one is now archaic and long overdue for burial. The Aireacht proposal was a brave attempt to reformulate and redefine the convention in terms appropriate to the latter part of the twentieth century. If that approach is not adopted, then some other attempt must be made to define and limit ministerial responsibility in such a way as to break the stranglehold which, in its present form, it has created for Ministers and for the civil service. I can offer no comprehensive solution to the problem. Perhaps a start might be made by a formal statement by the Taoiseach which limited a Minister's responsibility to 'serious' errors or omissions of his or her Department. The deficiencies of this approach are obvious. The statement could not set aside any legal liability that might arise. Moreover, how is 'serious' to be defined in practice? Nevertheless, it might be useful to have the principle firmly stated even if the content of that principle would become clear only in practice. This approach (as in the case of the Aireacht) would call for political determination and courage. It may well seem to be both undesirable and impracticable. There may of course be another way. But one thing is clear; doing nothing is not a solution.

The principle of *limited* ministerial responsibility has been enunciated on only one occasion, by Seán MacEntee, Minister for Health during the passage through the Dáil of the Mental Treatment (Detention in Approved Institutions) Bill in 1961.[13] On that occasion the Minister firmly — and rightly — refused to accept personal responsibility for the failure of a junior official to observe the regulations regarding the committal of persons to mental institutions. The Minister's statement was confined to the specific situation dealt with by the legislation. What I have in mind, as a first step, is a statement applicable to all Ministers, not confined to a specific situation.

In an acute comment made shortly after the Devlin Report was published, Professors Basil Chubb and Patrick Lynch pointed out that:

> The greatest achievement of Mr Devlin and his colleagues is to show how ministerial responsibility can be reconciled with a public service providing the kind of management that modern techniques make possible in enterprises, big and small. *One would have wished, however, that the concept of ministerial responsibility had been discussed more fully* (my italics) (Chubb and Lynch, 1969).

One thing is clear: the archaic aspect of the concept of ministerial responsibility is evidenced by the fact that it seems to have little practical application. In how many cases, if any, has it led to the resignation of a Minister? According to Chubb, eight Ministers resigned between 1922 and 1968 (Chubb, 1970) but, with one dubious exception (Eoin MacNeill over the Boundary Commission Report 1925), no resignation resulted from the application of the doctrine of ministerial responsibility. Neither was this doctrine responsible for any ministerial resignation since 1968 — I exclude from consideration in this context the 1970 changes connected with the 'Arms Trial'. I think we can dismiss as unlikely the contention that in the sixty years since the State was established no occasion arose which would have justified ministerial resignation, had the doctrine of ministerial responsibility been fully operational. It is difficult to disagree with Professor Finer's conclusion (in a British context) that '... a minister's resignation was only likely to be effected if he was willing to go, his prime minister was firm, and his own party was clamorous for his resignation'.[14] One may well wonder, however, what remains *in practice* of the doctrine of ministerial responsibility.

Only those who have worked close to Ministers have any idea of the many demands on their time. These demands reflect the variety of functions discharged by a Minister. He is a member of a political party, a parliamentary representative, a member of a Government and the political head of a Department. No attempt has been made to assess the amount of ministerial time devoted to each of these functions. My present concern is with the amount of time devoted to departmental duties. British studies suggest that this may be as low as 25 per cent (Kellner and Crowther-Hunt, 1980, 216). From personal experience I would think that this would be a reasonable approximation of the Irish position. One indication of the limited amount of time which a Minister can devote to the affairs of his Department is the difficulty which the *official* head of the Department (the secretary) and his senior colleagues experience in obtaining a meeting with him. Perhaps this difficulty is accentuated in the Department of Finance, whose Minister is subject to unusually varied pressures; it is certainly *not* a problem of personalities since the difficulty does not vary much with different Ministers. This factor supports the argument for divorcing policy from execution, for devoting to policy issues the limited time which the Minister can devote to departmental affairs.

The contention that civil servants have no function in relation to policy is, rightly, heard no more. Few would now quarrel with Seán Lemass's dictum that 'the responsibility of civil servants is to press matters to a conclusion. The responsibility of Government is to press matters to a decision'. What is less clear-cut is the extent to which this formulation involves civil servants in the political process — or, rather, the extent to which civil servants are, or should be, politically sensitive. I must confess to some scepticism on this point. I cannot associate myself with Nevil Johnson's statement that 'civil servant are the guardians of the political interests of Ministers' (Johnson, 1965). I would, however, reject as caricature the assertion (made in an *Irish* context) that: 'At the present time the attitude of most civil servants to anything vaguely political is one of virginal shock and horror' (Manning, 1975). On this issue I find myself in that least exciting of positions — the middle ground. There are few aspects of administration which are not politically sensitive; for civil servants to ignore this would be naive. But I contend that civil servants should not be over-concerned about the political consequences of their recommendations; these are best left to the politicians themselves. Sir William Harcourt's well-known dictum still holds good: 'The Minister exists to tell the civil servant what the public won't stand'.

I forget who first called civil servants political eunuchs — a description which may obscure the fact that the political impartiality on which western public administration is founded is basically a willingness to serve successive governments and, in effect, to work against successive oppositions. Impartiality is not neutrality; the civil servant works for the government of the day. Not enough attention has been given to the stress which in some circumstances this loyalty can impose on the civil service as a whole and on some individual civil servants. Commitment and dedication can suffer if there are abrupt and frequent reversals of policy; in administration, as in parliamentary democracy, there has to be respect for, and observance of, a minimum level of agreed conventions. Strain can also result from other factors. Thus a political utterance, clearly at variance with facts known to the civil servant, may not put his or her loyalty or silence at risk, but it can make civil servants sceptical of the political process.

It is sometimes contended that civil servants are insulated from the reality within which governments must act and that they should be exposed to the pressures which face Ministers. The employment of outside advisers is the response of those who, accepting that civil servants cannot be inserted into the political process, insist on the political process being inserted into administration; I turn to this issue later.

THE PERMANENT SECRETARY

Secretaries of departments — the 'principal officer', to use the terminology of the Ministers and Secretaries Acts — are appointed by the government. The normal procedure is that the appointment is made on the nomination of the Minister of the Department concerned. It is very seldom indeed that a Minister has not accepted the recommendation made by his officials, typically by the retiring secretary. I am not aware of any case where a Minister's nomination was *not* accepted by the government. It would indeed be surprising were it otherwise, for few members of the government would have an intimate knowledge of the second, or third level, officials in departments other than their own.

This is an unsatisfactory procedure.* It may be argued that the results to date do not justify changing it. I leave a judgement on that to others, while maintaining my view that the procedure is defective mainly because it enables undue weight to be given to seniority and because it does nothing to promote inter-departmental mobility. Perhaps we should take a leaf out of the British book in this subject. Our Department of the Public Service should monitor promotions at, say, the second and third highest levels in departments so as to identify the secretarial timber of the future, should promote inter-departmental mobility at this level and should be charged with advising the Taoiseach on the appointment of departmental secretaries. The Taoiseach would consult the Minister concerned, but the final word would rest with the Taoiseach. It is clear from the Crossman diaries that the appointment of permanent secretaries in Britain is both an open and a contentious issue — certainly not one where the outcome is regularly taken for granted.

Senior civil servants who might be in the running in the future for appointment as departmental secretaries will probably ask why I did not make this suggestion *before* I myself was appointed a departmental secretary. I have no answer to that.

As far as I am aware, the general civil service regulations apply in their entirety to departmental secretaries. This means, in particular, that the general provisions regarding retirement and superannuation apply to them without modification. In other words, there is no special provision for what might be called 'the burnt-out case' — the departmental secretary who, whether he has served too long or has found the pressures too heavy, is no longer able to function efficiently *as departmental secretary* i.e. as major policy adviser to his Minister and as the person with overall charge of the administration of the department. I have primarily in mind the first of these

---

*It has, in fact, been superseded by the appointment of the Top Level Appointments Committee.

responsibilities where it would hardly be surprising if, in some cases, peak performance were passed after a relatively short, though indeterminate, period. This point would gain added urgency if departmental secretaries were appointed at an earlier age than is customary, in recognition of the stresses of the job and of its demands in terms of initiative, detachment and original thinking. My point — a point which I first made many years ago — is that there may be cases where the national interest would be served if a departmental secretary were able to vacate his post, without financial hardship, before the ages of voluntary retirement (60 years) and compulsory retirement (65 years).[15] It is perhaps a sign of the times that a number of secretaries have retired before they reached 65 years but so, it must be admitted, do quite a number of other civil servants.

Enforced resignation is quite a different matter. There have to my knowledge been only two cases (McCarron, Local Government and Public Health, O'Donovan, Social Welfare) where deep-seated differences with Ministers led to enforced resignations of departmental secretaries. In a third case (Brennan, Finance) one might well wonder what would have happened had Brennan not been appointed Chairman of the Currency Commission in 1927; his differences with his Minister were such that he would hardly have continued as secretary (Fanning, 1978, 188-92).

Should departmental secretaries — and senior civil servants generally — consider that they have any responsibility to resign because they disagree fundamentally with government policy? This is a complex issue, but I have little hesitation in answering in the negative. However one quantifies the civil service input into policy-making, the ultimate responsibility for policy decisions rests with Ministers. If there is one factor which distinguishes the civil service from other institutions, it is their *duty* to serve different administrations and successive governments. This impartiality and continuity (which has been both admired and reviled) would be undermined if civil servants considered that they were obliged to record their disagreement with particular government policies by resigning. This conclusion applies equally to the apparently less draconian reaction of publicly criticising government policy, a point which has been lost on some commentators, for example: 'You have to keep coming back to things like NET; civil servants knew what was going on, but continued to do what their political masters told them'.[16]

I am predictably unhappy about press reports which state categorically that civil servants are worried about specific governmental or ministerial decisions. If the reports are true, and are 'leaks', they augur poorly for the civil service ethic of serving the Government of the day; if they are untrue, or if true, have been leaked by politicians, they place the service in an impossible position. The instructions for accounting officers (who are usually departmental secretaries) provide that where a Minister proposes to sanction expenditure which an accounting officer believes to be 'improper', the accounting officer should make the Minister aware of his reservations; if the Minister persists, the accounting officer should insist that the Minister overrides his objections in writing. Where a departmental secretary has grave reservations about a ministerial proposal, in circumstances where financial impropriety is not involved, he might be well advised to adopt a similar procedure, if he has not otherwise got a written 'discharge'. While I do not envisage that normally this 'discharge' would be published, this procedure might test the legal fiction that, in common with all civil servants, departmental secretaries hold office at the 'will and pleasure' of the government!

OUTSIDE ADVISERS

It is usually taken for granted that civil servants are hostile to outside advisers. As a generalisation this is clearly untrue since civil servants themselves have employed outside advisers. It is of course the employment by *Ministers* of outside advisers that has attracted public comment. While I suspect that the red carpet is rarely unfurled for these newcomers, I think that the civil service reactions fall far short of active hostility, indeed fall short of the belief attributed to them by Professor Chubb that 'the outsider probably has little to contribute' (Chubb, 1970). One danger to avoid is that of damaging the convention of civil service political impartiality. Too often the impression is given that it is necessary for Ministers to appoint outside advisers because they cannot 'rely' on the loyalty of the civil service. This is particularly the case when a government comes to power after a long period out of office. There was more than a hint of this when the Coalition Government assumed office in 1973;[17] it was particularly noticeable in relation to the Department of Finance, though not on the part of the Minister for Finance.

Sometimes accusations of inefficiency are coupled with doubts regarding the loyalty of the civil service as grounds for the appointment of advisers. In either case the appointment would, at best, be a short-term solution, although I accept that Ministers can justifiably retort that in the long-term they may be politically dead, long-term being defined as the period between now and the next election.

Although what discussion there has been in this country of this subject makes use of the term *cabinet,* our experience to date with outside advisers has fallen markedly short of the typical European ministerial *cabinet* in terms of status, numbers, and *modus operandi.* In one important respect, a misunderstanding regarding — or perhaps ignorance of — the French *cabinet* system (generally regarded as the prototype) may have contributed to some of the misunderstandings on the subject in Ireland. The typical member of a French *cabinet* is a civil servant, not an outsider. It is true that members of a French *cabinet* are closely associated with their Minister in a way which other civil servants are not. But the basis of selection is rarely political allegiance, and civil servants they remain even after 'their' Minister has left office; indeed they often serve in the *cabinet* of his successor. Most French departments have no equivalent of our departmental secretary and it is significant that, in the exceptional cases where there is such an equivalent, the *cabinet* has caused some friction. These are but some of the ways in which Irish civil service traditions (largely borrowed from Great Britain) differ from those found in other European civil services. Taken in conjunction with the conventions which have emerged over time, they help to explain why the *cabinet* system has become an effective part of the administrative system in France.

I would like to see some discussion in this country of the *cabinet* system. Part of the problem is the lack of agreement regarding what might be briefly described as 'the rules of the game'. We need to be clearer about these and also about what might reasonably be expected from such a system. No effort has been made to assess the successes and failures of the quasi-cabinet system adopted — or to identify the results which that system has achieved. It is to issues such as these that the discussion should be directed. In the absence of such a discussion, we must turn to British comments on the experience in that country with outside advisers or irregulars, to use the apt description of Samuel Brittan, himself a distinguished adviser in the Wilson Government in the sixties. Brittan has warned against the dangers of outsiders being too uncritical of Government policies and has suggested that, to avoid this, they should not have too strong a political commitment to the Government of the day. In a perceptive comment, he concluded that:

> Where many reformers, including the present writer, may have gone wrong in the past was in taking it for granted that it would be desirable to strengthen the influence of politicians against officials. The day-to-day horizons and public relations obsessions of most Ministers in any administration are no more worthy of reinforcement than the intellectual conservatism of most senior officials. Indeed in some ways the greatest criticism of conventional civil servants is that they let Ministers get away with too much nonsense, and do not sufficiently push forward unpalatable points of view. Yet at the same time Ministers are terribly in the hands of civil servants for the analysis of problems and the enumeration of practical policy alternatives. Such is the inwardness of the system that both these statements can be simultaneously true. Perhaps, at the root of it all is the view of the civil servant as a court eunuch who has his own special type of influence but must not presume to argue with his ministerial overlord on equal terms (Brittan, 1969).

On assuming office in 1964 Wilson showed a surprising reserve towards outside advisers (Wilson, 1964). He stressed that they

needed to be dovetailed into the administrative machinery —
'house trained' to use his own words; it is not clear whether
he was of the same view when he left office. Enoch Powell
has argued that a Minister should not be too immersed in the
affairs of the department and holds that there is no case for
an outside adviser when there is a junior minister in the
department who can act as a political backstop (Powell, 1964).

We do well to bear in mind, of course that the British
practice, no more than the Irish one, falls far short of the
European *cabinet* system. But British experience may be relevant
for as long as we continue to operate an ad-hoc, non-integrated
'system' of outside advisers. I readily accept that Ministers —
particularly new Ministers — may wish to be fortified by a
'political back-stop', to use Enoch Powell's phrase, and that
the civil service itself may benefit in the process, but I do not
see even a fully developed *cabinet* system, taken in isolation,
as making a decisive contribution to improving the administrative system, however much it may ease the workload on
Ministers.

IS THE CIVIL SERVICE A PROFESSION?

I find it difficult to get worked up about the question of
whether the civil service is, or is not a profession. Some of those
who talk in terms of the civil service being a profession stress
the responsibility of the profession for reforming the civil
service. I have no difficulty whatsoever in recognising, and
accepting, this responsibility, but cannot agree that it derives
from, or is augmented by, the allegedly professional nature of
the service. The Devlin Report was in no doubt on the issue:
'It is now time that the existence of a separate profession of
administration is formally recognised'. The Group did not
consider it necessary to elaborate this statement or to explain
what form the recognition would take or what significance
it would have.

Max Weber contended that the holding of public office is
a profession *per se*. For argument, as distinct from contention,
I turn to Thornley and Chubb: 'The civil service is generally
regarded as a profession and rightly so. It is one of the

distinguishing features of a profession that to a large extent it controls entry to its own ranks, guards its own standards and fosters its own science or art'.[18] It would not be too difficult to demonstrate that, on the basis of these three tests, the civil service is *not* a profession. Entry is determined by reference to legislation and ministerial regulations; breaches of standards are, in the extreme case, punished by dismissal enforced by the government; the civil service's record in regard to supporting the Institute of Public Administration does not demonstrate any marked zeal for fostering the science, or art, of public administration.

I find no more convincing Mary Follet's general definition: '. . . a profession is said to rest on the basis of an approved body of knowledge, and such knowledge is supposed to be used in the service of others, rather than merely for one's own purposes'. One might be tempted indeed, to regard this definition as mildly ironical ('. . . is said to rest . . . is supposed to be used . . .'). Leaving this aside, even Tom Barrington, from whom I take this quotation and who has underlined so strongly the professional responsibilities of the civil service, acknowledges that in relation to public administration, 'the concepts of science and service are of unequal strength' (Barrington, 1980).

As I have mentioned the Devlin Report in this context, it is fitting that (undeterred by Crossman's dismissal of the document as 'uninspired common sense') I should record what the Fulton Report has to say about the British civil service. Fulton talks of the professionalism of the civil servant, a professionalism defined as being skilled in one's job and having a fundamental knowledge of, and a deep familiarity with, a subject that enables a person to move with ease among its concepts. This approach is reminiscent of that of Sir Edward Bridges who discusses the *professional skill* of the civil service in terms of long experience, special techniques, a capacity and determination to study difficult subjects, and a disinterested desire for the truth (Bridges, 1953). Whether or not these noble attributes can be ascribed to the Irish civil service, can they be regarded as attributes of a profession, as that term is generally understood? I doubt it. I prefer the viewpoint of Sir William Armstrong, then head of the British civil service: 'We share some characteristics of the recognised professions, and not others; in some contexts the label is a useful shorthand, in others rather misleading' (Armstrong, 1970). With Sir William Armstrong, I prefer to be known as a (former) civil servant.

A misleading aspect of the professional label is the impression that is wrongly conveyed of collective responsibility, of collegiality, in the civil service. As I have already mentioned, I find this lacking even in the higher reaches of the service, where one might expect that it would be fostered if only by the fairly frequent business contact among a small group of senior officials.

Perhaps the crucial factor involved in the issue of professionalism is whether high standards are adopted and observed. I would hope that many civil servants would be counted among the company of those who suscribe to these noble aspirations — a company which I would not regard as being restricted to the professions, as traditionally defined.

THE PUBLIC IMAGE OF THE CIVIL SERVANT

Nearly forty years ago Clement Attlee wrote that 'the civil servant soon learns that sufferance is the badge of all his tribe' (Attlee, 1954). While Attlee was of course writing about the British civil service, his remarks apply also to the Irish civil service — and no doubt that of many other countries. Sufferance often takes the form of abuse, masquerading as criticism, sometimes tempered by praise, both often unjustified. A regrettable aspect of the abuse is that the reaction to it often ends in exaggerated protestations of virtue. Criticism, to use a more neutral term than abuse, is frequently well-merited and hopefully salutary. Much of it, however, is misconceived or could be met only by fundamental changes which are *not* envisaged by the critics.

The civil service is, for example, frequently criticised as a bureaucracy, for being *the* bureaucracy. Merely being a bureaucracy is a sufficient ground for criticism. But this criticism ignores the fact that the term covers much more than the civil service:

Sometimes bureaucracy seems to mean administrative efficiency, at times the opposite. It may appear as simple as a synonym for civil service, or it may be as complex as an idea summing up the specific features of modern organisational structure. It may refer to a body of officials, or to the routines of office administration. . . . The name 'bureaucracy' has been applied to: government by officials; public administration; the administration of any organisation; administrative efficiency or inefficiency; the modern organisation, to mention only some of the many concepts discussed. (Albrow, 1970).

According to Professor Chubb: 'The public service has two pervasive features: continuity and a relatively risk-free environment. Neither is especially good for lively government'. This may or may not be true but could the remedy not be worse than the disease? For example, in providing for discontinuity, can we be sure that we are not opening the door to patronage? It would be unwise to underestimate the attraction which appointments-at-will present to the politician.

In other cases, different voices speak with quite different tongues about the civil service. Weber declared that bureaucracy (admittedly a wider term than the civil service) makes democracy impossible. Attlee, however, regarded the impartiality of the civil service as 'one of the strongest bulwarks of democracy' (Atlee, *op. cit.,*) and the Rev. E.F. O'Doherty saw the impersonal civil servant as 'one of the great inventions of modern times' (O'Doherty, 1956).

Similar 'self-cancelling' comments can be cited. Chubb sees (rightly in my view) the subordinate role of the civil service as an important ingredient of democracy (Chubb, 1970) while Pyne considers that subordination may have gone too far (Pyne, 1974). Professor Lee regards civil servants as the parasites of our land (Lee, 1978) (recalling Marx's denunciation of bureaucrats as state parasites, richly paid sycophants and sinecurists), Brendan Halligan dismisses the service as effete decadence[19] and *Irish Business* contends that 'failure to reform the civil service explains much of what's wrong with the country to-day'.[20] Bruce Arnold, however, regards the service as 'the single most powerful institution in the country

. . . [which] will have to play the central decisive role in the tackling of the critical challenges the country faces'.[21] Ivor Kenny considers the civil service to be a powerful and sheltered interest group[22] while Bishop Philbin regards prudence, justice, fortitude and temperance as a prescription for the civil servants as well as for the saint (Philbin, 1960).

As I have said, much of the comment on the civil service, whether in criticism or praise, is not well-founded; the wisest course is to ignore it. This may at times call for a stoicism bordering on the virtuous — as for example when Seán MacBride virtually accused the Department of Finance of being engaged in 'deliberate sabotage' (Fanning, 1978) and of regarding 'a high rate of unemployment as necessary and desirable'.[23] There is, however, a danger of the 'self-conforming stereotype'. There is also the danger that the civil service may find intolerable, and react unfavourably and negatively to, a continued stream of ill-founded criticism, often bordering on abuse. It is easier to draw attention to the danger than to prescribe a remedy. In fact I do not believe that, at the end of the day, it will be possible to achieve a 'neutral' image for the civil service — neutral as between undeserved abuse on the one hand and equally undeserved praise on the other. Leaving aside abuse and praise, the service has for years been an object of fun; perhaps the best that can be hoped for is that the fun will be innocent. We should perhaps be content with a public attitude which, to paraphrase Rupert Brooke, is that:

> civil servants rarely smile
> being urban, squat and full of guile.

If the fun is to be kept at that, then civil servants will have to be more active than they have been in remedying the legitimate grievances of the public, and in removing, in so far as lies within their power, the cause of their poor image.

WHY THE IMAGE IS POOR

Some of the reasons why civil servants are held in poor repute are outside their own control. Thus part of the frustration and resentment against high and growing taxation is diverted to those who administer the taxes or the services paid for by taxation. Despite the growth of the public service, those who wrongly consider that they are entitled to more take out their grievance on the people whose function it is to reject their claims. Individuals dissatisfied with the Government vent their dissatisfaction on the civil service. The public are particularly incensed at what they regard as the excessive pay and pensions and job security of the administrators.

Much of the criticism of the civil service comes from what I believe to be a grossly exaggerated conception of the power of the service. Those who regard the service as 'the real (or permanent) Government' do not — rightly — regard this description as praise; if the description were regarded as true and praiseworthy, the implications for parliamentary democracy would indeed be serious. But it is significant that this terminology is usually adopted when discussing a development regarded by the commentator as undesirable. Thus it was the civil service, the 'real government' which axed the Tuam sugar beet factory, the Connaught Regional Airport. . . . It is, of course, the 'nominal' Government which dispenses the good things of life!

It would be stupid to suggest that civil servants are not in part the authors of their own misfortune as far as their public image is concerned. I would hold this to be true even in regard to one particular source of confusion and hostility, namely the lack of informed public discussions about the service. The service is so large and so little is known about it that it is hardly surprising that many of the public fear and hate what to them is unknown, a riddle, wrapped in a mystery, inside an enigma, to borrow Churchill's phrase. Without submitting to the theory that to know all is to forgive all, I maintain that the service has an obligation to inform the public of what it is about — whether or not this improves their image. They should bear in mind the words of Dean Swift: 'Providence never intended to make the management of public affairs a mystery to be comprehended by a few persons of sublime genius'.

The myriad services and numerous taxes administered by the civil service affect hundreds of thousands of individuals each year. It would be surprising if every one of these individuals were happy with the treatment they receive. It would be amazing if the poor image of the service were not in part the result of the justified frustration and anger of these individuals — justified not because their claims were rejected but rather by how their claims were handled. I know of no development more apt to improve the image of the civil service and, more important, to raise the standard of public administration than an improvement in the *quality* of services provided to the public. By quality I have in mind such factors as courtesy, consideration, information and speed. I single out the last mentioned as a particular concern of mine. Sometimes I think that an old Irish saying was devised with only the civil service in mind: when God made time, he made plenty of it. Time is certainly relative in this context: a letter which is unanswered for a week is, as far as the sender is concerned, a letter unanswered for a month. 'Delay in Whitehall is a major scandal', said Sir Edmund Compton before his appointment as the first ombudsman in Great Britain; he hoped that, as ombudsman, he would be able to do something about it.

It is ironical that the proposal to establish the office of ombudsman in this country provides as good as example as any of delay in the public sector — I use the wider term deliberately since the Dáil also was involved. The Devlin Report, published in September 1969, recommended the establishment of a commissioner for administrative justice. Six years passed before a private member's motion in favour of establishing the office of ombudsman was passed by the Dáil. An all-party informal committee (of the Dáil and Seanad) on administrative justice reported in favour of an ombudsman in May 1977. A bill was introduced by the Government in 1979 and passed into law in June 1980. The appointment of an ombudsman was (further) deferred as one of the July 1982 economy measures. Hardly an outstanding example of commitment and speed, even allowing for the many changes of government since 1969.

I believe that the cause of administrative reform would be well served by a system which provided that cases of notable delay would be selected for public examination with a view to identifying and analysing the factors responsible for the delay. But in accordance with my strongly held belief that institutional change by itself is unlikely to be effective, this suggestion should be accompanied by vigorous follow-up action to eliminate the causes of delay.

Delay in the civil service can be due to a number of factors such as sheer inefficiency, failure to relate resources to demands, indifference or (more probably) insensitivity to the legitimate demands of the public, an inability to put oneself in the other person's shoes.

These faults are not of course unique to the civil service and it would be unwise of the private sector to adopt a holier-than-thou attitude. Furthermore, to equate the civil service solely with delay would be a grotesque caricature of reality. I am aware of impossible deadlines met, of work done with speed and efficiency without regard for the sacrifice of private time or convenience. I am aware, also, of other examples (e.g. in relationship to membership of the EEC and EMS) where new and complex tasks were tackled with commendable dispatch. Over three hundred years ago, a British civil servant, Samuel Pepys, made an entry in his diary which rings a bell with many civil servants today: 'Late at the office. Home, with my mind full of business, and so to bed'.

SQUARING THE CIRCLE

Some criticisms of the civil service, if accepted, would call for a fundamental change in the service. It is far from clear that the critics realise or accept this. I am not necessarily arguing against the need for change, but merely stressing that the discussion is often incomplete.

Take, for example, the well-known exhortation by Seán Lemass that departments should regard themselves as development corporations (Lemass, 1961). Lemass did not spell out what he had in mind; the speech in which he advanced this concept is tantalisingly brief on this subject. Although the concept has since been referred to many times, no one has spelt out the implications e.g. for risk-taking. The essence of development is taking risks, of calculating chances. Someone has said that in business if you are right 51% of the time, you're successful. Would the public accept this test, or even a somewhat stricter one, in regard to departments of state? I see no reason why they shouldn't. I know many civil servants who would welcome such an approach. But I am not sure if Ministers, the Oireachtas and the public generally would welcome, or are prepared for, such a change. Just to take one aspect, the whole doctrine of ministerial responsibility would have to be rewritten if the concept of departments as development corporations were put into full operation. I have already argued that the doctrine is archaic and needs to be rewritten *in any event* but, although archaic, it still exists.

To take another example, the civil service is frequently criticised because it provides risk-free, permanent jobs. It is, incidentally, ironical that, in strict law, a civil servant's position must be one of the most insecure in the country; he holds office 'at the will and pleasure' of the Government and has not, for example, the benefit of the Unfair Dismissals Act. This is one of the fictions that has confused the public (another example is ministerial responsibility) since it is undeniable that the law and practice have parted company many, many decades ago. Do the critics wish the practice to conform to the law? Economically it would be quite costly; civil servants would demand compensation for the loss of security. Politically, by opening the door to a change to top jobs, if not more, on a change of government, it would strike at the tenet of civil service impartiality and would result in damaging uncertainty and gross inefficiency. A far less draconian solution lies to hand — a system of promotion in which a predominant weight is given to merit and to initiative. I am well aware, from personal experience, that this solution is much more difficult than it seems, mainly because of the difficulty of devising an objective, convincing test of merit — convincing, that is, to the non-promotee. Mere enunciation of this 'good' is not enough; the bland recommendation in the Devlin Report was particularly uninspiring and less than helpful.

But to revert to my main theme and to take yet another aspect. Civil servants are often (and rightly) accused of being inflexible, of going by the book, of not using their judgement. There is substance in much of this criticism, but are the critics prepared to accept the consequences if action were taken to meet it? Flexible judgement means that different civil servants may treat individuals in similar circumstances differently; if this is not acceptable, a costly system of surveillance may be required. The critics may regard this as acceptable and I would not argue with them — my point is that the criticism has not been thought through.

Flexibility on issues not involving individual entitlements brings me back to the familar issue of risk-taking, or what might appear to be risk-taking. For example: a decade or so ago, a D-Mark Loan was raised at a time when all the indications were that the D-Mark was about to be revalued. The Department of Finance postponed for some days converting the proceeds of the loan into Irish Pounds (having satisfied itself that it had the powers to do so) and in a short while made a profit of about £¾ million for the Exchequer. The Comptroller and Auditor General queried the Department's legal powers to delay paying the proceeds into the Central Fund, and reported this aspect to the Public Accounts Committee. Whatever legal doubt there was (the Department denied there was any) was subsequently removed by legislation; but in the meantime an outsider could well be excused for thinking that the Exchequer had been prejudiced by, rather than had benefited from, this minor exercise in flexibility.

The question of civil service anonymity provides my last example of how the critics have not always thought through their criticism. I am not talking here of dealings with individual members of the public, where I am glad to see increasing emphasis on the need to personalise such dealings. I have in mind the criticism that policy is made by 'faceless' civil servants, who are not publicly accountable for the results. The critics contend that the civil servants who make policy should be named so that the public would at least know 'the face behind the policy'. It is, of course, true that civil service anonymity has long been breached; some civil servants — generally to their chagrin — are as well known as some well-advertised detergents. The more this trend continues, the greater will be the clamour that civil servants should be held accountable for policy decisions. The demand has already been made that 'when civil servants effectively make policy by Ministerial default, they must become publicly accountable for their actions'.[24]

Any self-respecting politician would rightly object to this, even where accountability carried undertones of odium but all the more so where some credit was to be gained. Even acknowledging — as I do without reservation — the significant contribution which civil servants make to policy formulation, to hold civil servants accountable for policy would inevitably lead to disclosure of those cases where policy was *not* in accord with civil service advice. Advocates of 'open' government might welcome this, but the development would strike at the root of minister/civil service relationships and conventions and also, I suggest, at the role of the civil service in the process of parliamentary democracy. This might or might not be desirable; my point is that we should be sure of what lies at the end of the road before we set foot on it.

CONCLUSION

As I wrote at the outset, this is a highly selective paper. It is also a disjointed one and therefore difficult to summarise. Let me, instead, conclude with some very general comments.

I do not share the view of those who consider that the civil service is inimical to the process of parliamentary democracy. On the contrary, I hold that the service is an indispensable but of course a subordinate element in that process. I believe that this factor alone (there are others) places a heavy responsibility on the civil service to be innovative and to be zealous in serving the public. I accept (I have no option!) that much remains to be done; indeed in certain respects little has yet been achieved, though not for want of trying. Despite this, I contend that the public criticism of the service tends more towards abuse than fair comment. In part this reflects and in part has contributed towards the increasing cynicism about politics and public affairs which has been so pronounced in recent years. This cynicism is indeed so marked that I am not sure what my advice would be to any person contemplating the civil service as a career.

But that is defeatist thinking. I prefer to think that things can and will change. Whether change will come, or whether it will come quickly enough, from a continuation of present policies I have considerable reservations. Specifically, I have doubts whether 'staying with Devlin' will be any more successful in the future than in the past. Even more specifically, we should drop the Aireacht proposal if resolute action in the next year or so has not moved it out of the doldrums.[25] The time has come to place more emphasis on personnel policies, including the critical factor of inter-departmental mobility. I suspect that the Department of the Public Service has accepted this. But until there is a much greater commitment to change I do not believe that shifting from one emphasis to another will make all that much difference. How to secure and maintain that commitment? I have no easy answer. But I am convinced that commitment will not be forthcoming unless political and administrative fortunes are made dependent on the success or failure of administrative reform. Unless that happens, we may as well forget about change, and regard the civil service as a 'grand and achieved result' rather than as 'a working and changeable instrument'.

3

Irish Government Further Observed

This article first appeared in Administration *Vol. 31, No. 3, 1983*

ADMINISTRATIVE REFORM: POLITICAL COMMITMENT

Administrative reform is much in the air — at least in the political air. Before, during, and after the second General Election of 1982, the air was thick with promises, commitments and threats to reform public administration. The then government's *The Way Forward — National Economic Plan 1983-1987* promised that 'the continuing relevance of the Devlin Committee approach to public sector reform will be reviewed by a small Committee of selected Departmental Secretaries and private sector experts with a view to making specific recommendations to improve efficiency in working methods, accountability and management in the public sector'.

Fine Gael's *Policy for Economic Recovery* denounced the failure to implement key aspects of the 1969 Devlin Report 'as one of our real political scandals' and believed that 'we should act now to put its remaining major recommendations into effect'. Included in these was 'The ending of the myth that a Minister is responsible for every act of a civil servant...'[26] This theme was repeated by John Bruton, TD, in a pre-election statement of 'The Issues' in which he stated that 'A central issue is, therefore, the reform of the Civil Service. I believe the Devlin Report, published in 1969, should be implemented in full'.[27] A post-election *Programme for Government* by Fine Gael and

Labour committed the parties to establishing the office of Ombudsman and to a reform of the public service designed to secure maximum efficiency, mobility of staff, open competitions for certain civil service jobs and the employment of outside help as may be necessary.[28]

It is too soon yet* to assess what results have been achieved, or to establish what significance should be attached to the fact that the new Minister for the Public Service is the first holder of that post who is not also responsible for another portfolio, be it Finance or Labour. This development marks yet another break with the recommendations of the Public Service Organisation Review Group whose report (the Devlin Report) recommended that the two portfolios of Public Service and Finance should be held by the one person. Time has proved that, whatever the theoretical advantage of this recommendation, the demands of the Finance portfolio are too exacting to permit the holder to pay adequate attention to another portfolio. Indeed, these demands are such that the Minister for Finance should not alone not be burdened with another portfolio, but should have the assistance of two Ministers for State. One of these should be responsible for economic and social planning; the other, responsible for controlling public expenditure, should have continuous discussions throughout the year with other ministers — the effort involved in containing expenditure requires no less. True to my Finance antecedents, I would argue these two appointments should not add to the total number of Ministers for State; corresponding reductions can and should be made elsewhere.

Reverting to my main theme, the importance and urgency of public sector reform certainly warrants the undivided attention of a minister. It is to be hoped that the results will justify this viewpoint. My main reservation relates to the separation of public sector pay, which accounts for some 50 per cent of current public expenditure (excluding service of public debt) from the direct control of the minister responsible for the Budget. A transfer of this responsibility to the

---

*This paper was written in March 1983. Changes in the system of appointments to senior posts in the civil service were announced in January 1984.

Department of Finance might make more effective both the budgetary process and the process of public sector reform.

What has happened to public sector reform is a classical example of the clash between the urgent and the important — typically (as in this case) a one-sided clash in which the 'musts' take pride of place before the 'oughts', to use Tom Barrington's phrase. We are faced now with the consequences of having, over many years, put off until tomorrow what we thought need not be done today. Let there be no doubt about it, public sector reform is a long-term affair. The temptation, on that account, to afford it a low priority is strong. But problems in this area tend to increase with neglect rather than remain static. We are confronted today with the long-term consequences of past neglect, and of resort to short-term expediencies.

ADMINISTRATIVE REFORM: POLITICAL FRAMEWORK

Public administration does not operate in a political vacuum. The political framework within which Irish public administration works has been characterised in recent years by electorate cynicism and disenchantment, the product of such factors as:

> the politics of promises which either have not been delivered or have been delivered at too high a price;
> the apparent inability to make reasonable progress in solving such major national problems as unemployment, inflation and external imbalance;
> the lack of credibility in fiscal policy as witnessed by the failure to deliver on the repeated commitments by different governments to wipe out the budget deficit over a few years;
> the perceived irrelevance of the Dáil and Seanad and the growing power of pressure groups.

Over and above these, and many other, factors, I suspect that cynicism and disenchantment flow from the realisation that government has become too large, is attempting too much, is getting out of control. Coupled with this — indeed a main causal factor — is the tendency for governments to assume responsibilities which they are not capable of discharging because of external and internal factors outside their control. As against this, governments tend to claim credit for favourable developments (a fall in inflation resulting from a reduction in import prices, for example) which are due to factors not of their making. It is only right to admit, however, that, if our governments attempt too much, we, in turn, demand too much from them. It is hard to know which is cause and which effect.

The political process is not enhanced when the participants themselves, in dismissing their opponents' argument, accuse them of 'playing politics' with the issue; the only worse accusation in this creed is that of 'playing party politics'.

IMPLICATIONS FOR PARLIAMENTARY DEMOCRACY

The growth and complexity of the public sector has long undermined the doctrine of ministerial responsibility for all departmental activities, although there has been a strange reluctance to accept all the implications of this erosion. But it has done more than this. In terms of the demands made by the system, it has tilted the balance between public servant and minister, and tilted it in favour of the public servant. It has significantly extended the time required by a minister to become familiar enough with his or her department to enable major policy changes to be formulated. It has thus extended the time required by a new government to devise new policies and significantly alter underlying economic and social trends.

It is doubtful if the normal life of a government of four years or so is now adequate for the preparation and implementation of national plans. The short lives of recent governments have reminded us painfully that the parliamentary democratic process must be capable of providing governments with the minimum life required for effective policy-making and implementation. This 'efficiency argument' points to the advisability of providing, by statute, that parliament should have a fixed, rather than a maximum, life of five years. This would not necessarily mean that governments would have a correspondingly fixed life of five years, but it could be a significant step in that direction. There are, of course, arguments against fixed-life parliaments, but other countries operate such a system and it could hardly raise more difficulties for us than the present one.

The doctrine of parliamentary control of the executive was already considerably weakened before the explosive growth of the public sector in recent years. It has been further emasculated by that growth. The critical role of Opposition parties has also been undermined.

I am not sure that these problems would be significantly eased by the provision of more information about the public sector. I am not arguing for or against further information. What I am contending is that the growth and complexity of the public sector have introduced new time lags and nuances into the parliamentary democracy-public administration axis. They have, in addition, made politics and the public sector distant, remote, and mystifying to the ordinary citizen.

These are some of the reasons why I am led to the conclusion that, in terms of public administration, Big is Ugly and Small is Beautiful, and that an excessively large public sector and parliamentary democracy do not mix well. In the striking imagery of Tom Barrington:

> It is as if an ice floe were to crack and break, leaving government on the one part and governed on the other, each drifting steadily, inexorably apart (Barrington, 1982).

Our problem is not, of course, unique. A perceptive study of western democracies concluded that:

> Many observers have seen in the clash of these two trends (mass enfranchisement and the growth of state responsibilities) the 'axial problem' of modern society (Aberbach, Putnam and Rockman, 1981).

It may well be doubted whether public sector reform will be fully effective if the present size of the public sector has to be taken as given; the doubts increase as the sector continues to grow. The irony is that the bigger the public sector, the greater the need for reform.

Public sector reform is now big business, not only because of the benefits it can bestow, in terms of efficiency, consumer satisfaction, tax reliefs, etc., but also because of the problems which failure to reform poses for parliamentary democracy. It is the implication of size for parliamentary democracy, and for the conventions on which it rests, that concern me. I have particularly in mind the relations between ministers and senior public servants, in regard to policy formulation and decision-making, and, in turn, the relations between ministers and parliament. Big government can tend to blur, if not remove, the line which divides the politician from the bureaucrat, in particular the line which marks the division of functions in regard to policy formulation, decision and execution. It took us many years to accept that bureaucrats are involved in policy making, but in a subordinate role — formulating, not deciding, policy.

Commentators elsewhere, observing the growth of government, have speculated that the role of politicians and bureaucrats may be converging, 'perhaps reflecting, as some have argued, the politicisation of the bureaucracy and the bureaucratisation of the politician'. They have drawn attention to the problems and dangers of this process:

> The moral dilemma posed by bureaucratic policy making is power without responsibility; the dilemma of policy making by politicians is power without competence. Excessively bureaucratic policy making may lead to a crisis of legitimacy, but excessive political policy making threatens a crisis of effectiveness (*ibid*).

I think that we are far from that stage in Ireland, although our slowness in the past to admit that the bureaucrat had any role in the making of policy suggests that I could be wrong in this. But it is undeniable that big government has many implications for the ministerial-civil servant relationship. By making the politician's job more complex and technical, it adds emphasis to an old controversy — what training should the politician receive for the job? Should politics be a life-time career? Are we prepared to pay politicians on that basis? There has been misrepresentation and evasion on this subject. The politicians themselves have been mainly to blame, being reluctant to take a firm stance. The media have not always been helpful in ensuring an informed and responsible discussion on this critical issue.

Ireland inherited from Britain a public administrative system in which the gulf between civil servants and politicians is possibly greater than in most other comparable countries. There is no institutional cross-walk between the two worlds in this country, and the few individuals who have crossed over have (to mix the metaphor) jumped over the wall. The contrast between the two worlds is not so marked in other countries. A study of western democracies concluded that:

> Indeed, comparatively speaking, the Anglo-American democracies are quite unusual in the relative insignificance of the bureaucratic channel into the political elite *(ibid.)*.

An earlier study had shown that:

> In the Netherlands . . . 24 per cent of the Ministers came from the higher civil service and 20 per cent from the army. Under the French Fifth Republic, more than half the Ministers have been chosen from top level civil servants who thus became full-fledged politicians (Mattei, 1975).

It would be fascinating to explore the influence which our marked distinction between politician and bureaucrat has had on our political and administrative systems. One thing seems clear; the distinction has helped to raise the status of ministers and to increase the deference paid to them by public administrators. The public service is a markedly hierarchical system (a feature it shares with other bureaucracies) and the minister, as the last link in the chain, is the apex in the hierarchy — mixed metaphors notwithstanding.

CONSULTATION AND THE SEARCH FOR CONSENSUS

The business of government is to promote and implement policies which the electorate approves or is prepared to accept.

A wise government seeks to establish the electorate's preferences by, inter alia, a process of consultation. As government grows in size, consultation becomes even more necessary if government is not to become arbitrary or ignorant, or both. But a price has to be paid for consultation, and, as in other walks of life, a balance has to be struck between costs and benefits. The benefits are often obvious enough, but not so such costs as decisions unduly or indefinitely deferred, and excessive demands on the time of people in the private and public sectors. The need for balance is particularly great when the process of consultation develops into a search for consensus.

Perhaps I might illustrate my point by reference to the National Economic and Social Council (NESC) on which I served from its establishment in 1973 to the end of 1981. NESC has a membership of some forty-six persons representative of employers, trade unions, farmers, government departments and 'independents'. It has issued sixty-eight reports on a wide variety of topics; virtually all its recommendations have been unanimous. A formidable, indeed impressive, achievement. In terms of results, however, the picture is different. Making all allowance for:

1. the time-lag between recommendation-decision-implementation, and
2. the difficulty, when many voices are speaking, of ascribing credit to NESC recommendations for specific government actions,

the fruit of sixty-eight NESC reports, involving close on two million words, is unimpressive*. If this judgement seems harsh, let me recall that I was a member of the Council for most of its life to date. Nor should my comment be read as rejection of tri-partite discussions and the search for consensus. But where the discussions and the search have yielded such disappointing results, with such enormous demands on the resources of the private and public sectors, then the time is overdue for a reassessment, not of the *objectives,* but rather of the *procedures,* of consensus. Too many people spend too much

---

*I am glad to acknowlede that NESC's performance improved significantly in the 1980s.

time on too many issues to little avail. The search for consensus has too often resulted in delay or inaction. It is true that minds have been broadened, but often at the expense of a shirking of governmental responsibility for policy decision and implementation.

It is true also — to take the NESC once again — that many useful reports have been prepared, often on important issues not previously documented. A job well done indeed — but not the job that was envisaged.

It is indeed ironic that concerns were expressed in the past that the search for consensus might bystep parliament, might dilute the democratic process. Almost twenty years ago the present Taoiseach [Garret FitzGerald] considered that:

> In practice we now have a vocational-bureaucratic system of government whose centre of gravity has shifted away from the politician towards the civil service and vocational bodies.[29]

In fact matters have worked out otherwise. God knows where the centre of gravity is — but, if the power to influence decisions is the test, it is certainly not in these representative bodies. I fully accept that this assessment may reflect my personal experience of the consensus approach and may be unduly influenced by that experience. Perhaps this is but one of the many issues that would benefit from some research.

Bodies like NESC could be described as standing advisory bodies with very wide terms of reference, as distinct from ad hoc advisory bodies, with specific terms of reference. The history of the public service, and of government, is littered with the names of such bodies, but hardly with the fruit of their work. It would be difficult to rebut the old jibe that these bodies are created when a respectable reason is sought for doing nothing. There has been a welcome tendency in recent years to ease the heavy demands which these bodies make on the time and goodwill of their members. I have in mind such innovations as the engagement of consultants by the Public Services Organisation Review Group, and the appointment of a paid full-time Chairman to the Commission on Taxation. Whether the record in regard to results will be any better remains to be seen. The auguries are not promising.

BUDGETARY POLICY AND ECONOMIC PLANNING

Whatever benefits have been derived from the process of consultation and consensus, few would argue that the process has helped to ease the budgetary problems which have troubled us for so long, and show every sign of continuing to trouble us for years to come. Budgetary problems, in turn, are closely related to two other national issues — balance of payments deficits and inflation — and indirectly to a third — unemployment. National economic planning, if it is to be consistent, has to address itself to these four issues. This does not necessarily mean that each should be given equal priority or that the time-scale for action should be the same in each case. It *does* mean striking a consistent, acceptable and realistic balance between each. It was the failure to do this which — more than anything else — bedevilled the efforts at national economic planning in this country. This failure was particularly noticeable in regard to the current and the capital budgets and was particularly reprehensible because, however difficult the problems, they were at least somewhat more amenable to government control than the others. It is difficult to have economic plans taken seriously when the government does not take seriously those 'obligations' which are most relevant to it.

Of course changing circumstances may dictate departures from planned medium-term budgetary dispositions, but consistency and credibility require that some attempt be made to justify such departures.

I am not laying all the blame for planning failures on these departures, nor am I suggesting that other public sector aspects, e.g., the lack of administrative reform, were not contributory factors. But I am in no doubt about the importance of budgetary lapses.

I referred earlier to credibility. Government credibility in regard to budgetary policy — and indeed generally — has, I submit, been damaged by the failure to observe repeated commitments to reduce the current budget deficit within a few (or stated number of) years. Happiness is, by no means, a balanced budget, but we have found in the past eleven years that imbalanced budgets do not solve our problems. Not least amongst the unfortunate results of this weak, wavering approach to budgetary policy has been the confusing comments to which it has given rise. Thus, in the controversy as to whether the budgetary deficit should be phased out over a four *or* five year period, the argument *against* the shorter period tends to take the form that 'there are good economic arguments why balancing the tax and spending books should not be observed religiously in the midst of a recession.'[30] As if adoption of the shorter period amounted to balancing the books!

THE SELF-INTERESTED CIVIL SERVANT

Some commentators see the public sector as a major pressure group, responsible in large part for the growth of public expenditure and, by inference, a major obstacle to public sector reform. Those who argue on these lines tend to regard the public bureaucrat as being actuated mainly by self-interest, as seeking, in the language of the economist, to maximise his or her personal utility.

If we are to believe Tullock:

> It is not from the benevolence of the bureaucrat that we expect our research grant or our welfare check, but out of his regard to his own, not the public, interest (Jackson, 1982).

Given the extent to which the public sector is trade-unionised, it would be foolish to argue that Irish public servants are indifferent to self-interest. Leaving aside the question whether they are more, or less, self-interested than those in the private sector, the important issue is whether this self-interest, by increasing public expenditure, makes the reform of the public service more difficult.

Niskanen, a leading advocate of the theory of the self-interested bureaucrat, contends that:

> bureau outputs (i.e., public budgets) are greater than those which are socially optimal (*ibid.*, 131)

so much so, indeed that:

> the size of the public sector, and hence the amount of taxes paid, will be up to twice the social optimum *(ibid)*.

Niskanen's theories have been advanced to explain the growth of Irish public expenditure. Moore McDowell cites Niskanen with qualified approval in coming to the conclusion that:

> There are, therefore, reasons to believe, a priori, that the economic self-interest of those employed in the public sector can help explain its growth (McDowell, 1982).

Other Irish economists have said much the same. Thus Dr Kieran Kennedy has stated that:

> The supply of public services also creates its own bureaucracy with a strong vested interest in maintaining and expanding its own programme (Kennedy, 1982).

Niskanen's theories have not escaped criticism by his fellow economists. It would be foolish of an ex-administrator to be caught in a cross-fire between economists, but I cannot resist some quotations from a recent work by P. M. Jackson which suggest that care should be taken in generalising from Niskanen. According to Jackson, criticism of Niskanen:

> amounts to saying that an understanding of the effects of alternative incentive structures are important for any explanation of bureaucratic behaviour (Jackson, *op. cit.,* 134).

Niskanen's approach 'tends to wash out politics from the analysis and the influence of interest groups, etc., on the choice of policies' *(ibid.,* 133).

Finally, (and, perhaps, most tellingly) Niskanen's model:

> is the product of his own introspection and experiences as a bureaucrat, operating within a particular institutional environment, and within a specific culture at a single moment in time. Variations in the cultural and institutional settings, along with changes in the time period, will provide different conclusions *(ibid.,* 133).

Rejection of the Niskanen model of the self-centred bureaucrat does not involve acceptance of the model of the selfless public servant . . . 'a sort of monk who forsook all earthly pleasures and all personal happiness in order to serve' (*ibid.*). The preferences, convictions and prejudices of public servants are by no means irrelevant in explaining the growth of public expenditure. There is a natural tendency to become involved in the organisation in which one works; where commitment ends, and over-involvement (a form of administrative jingoism) begins, varies from individual to individual. However, to accept the proposition that the public sector as a whole is hell-bent on extending the services it provides involves accepting a degree of self-interest and over-involvement by public servants, and a weakness in the system of checks and balances, which strain credulity.

THE NEED FOR ADMINISTRATIVE RESEARCH

A theme underlying much of this article (and also my article on A Working and Changeable Instrument) is the close link between administrative reform and applied administrative research — applied in the sense that its lessons are put into effect. Research is not, of course, a condition sufficient for reform, but it can help to tease out the many issues involved, can direct effort where it will be most effective, and can help in securing the cooperation and support of the public service.

There is no shortage of candidates for administrative research. Top of my list are the causes of, and remedies for, delay in the public sector. Close to it — if not competing for first place — is an analysis of the attitude of the higher civil service towards administrative reform. Both of these are complex topics, raising far-reaching and interacting issues. An important by-product of such research would be the insight it would provide on the origin and background of higher civil servants. For too long reliance in this respect has been placed on the excellent, but outdated, work of Sean O'Mahony (Ó Mathúna, 69-74). Academics deserve better than this!

Administrative research would not alone help towards

greater efficiency, but would also provide a basis for objective, scholarly criticism of the administrative system — a most necessary input to the process of reform. Some assessments of the public service seem to portray a willingness to pass judgement without benefit of the facts, to proceed from a doubtful hypothesis to a confident, and often critical, conclusion. Criticism may well be deserved, but one would wish that it were based on facts rather than on speculation.

More administrative research might provide a basis for informed, critical, academic comment and thus lead to a better public understanding of the public service. But research is not an end in itself, and will only be useful if the lessons it points to are applied — and seen to be applied. To take an example — which is not research in the strict meaning of the term, but is, nevertheless, an excellent example of objective, critical examination of administrative institutions. I am referring to the reports of the Joint Oireachtas Committee on State-sponsored Bodies. To date the Committee has completed nineteen reports in the period since it got into its stride in mid-1978. Whether one agrees or not with individual reports and specific recommendations, one must acknowledge without reservation that this hardworking Committee is doing an excellent job. No doubt these reports have had some effect on the state-sponsored bodies and departments concerned. Yet we lack firm evidence of this. We lack also an overview of the role and future of the Committee. Hardly surprising, since none of its reports has been debated in the Dáil or Seanad. But surprising, nevertheless, when one recalls that for some twenty years, if not indeed more, before it was established there was strong and sustained pressure for such a Committee — generally from whatever party was in opposition!

Another subject which needs to be researched is Planning-Programme-Budgeting Systems. Here was a new, complex development initiated by the Department of Finance involving a vast amount of training and induction. Many departments were involved, new techniques learned, new expertise (and experts) acquired. All in all, much time, money and individual effort and enthusiasm were expended. Yet, while the system was still in its early stages, it was deferred indefinitely, although departments were encouraged to retain and operate specific operational parts of it (e.g. management information systems). There are valuable lessons to be learnt from the failure of this experiment, but they will not be learnt until they are teased out by research. This is not an academic issue. The problems which PPBS sought to tackle are still with us — indeed have increased enormously since the experiment was first conceived. We need to know why the experiment failed, how much of it could/should be salvaged, what lessons can be learnt from the failure in devising an alternative approach. From my involvement — admittedly limited — with the experiment, I know some of the answers, but these differ, apparently, from those known to outside commentators. Chubb, for instance, refers to the project as having been 'quietly dropped', (Chubb, 1980) which is hardly a complete account, while Barrington says that:

> Various techniques — capital appraisal, cost benefit, programming, planning budgeting — to improve the sophistication of appraisal were tried and because they did not fulfil (excessive) expectations were, like the toys of a wanton child, simply thrown away, leaving an inadequate legacy of disciplined thinking (Barrington, 1982).

A harsher viewpoint than that reflected in his earlier comment that:

> In Ireland these (PPBS) too, after a promising start, have largely fallen victims to the blight that affects so many initiatives for the development of our systems of public administration (Barrington, 1980).

A final comment on administrative research. If the paucity of research is a cause of concern, so too is the basis on which research is funded. I have in mind particularly the way in which the Exchequer funds research undertaken by the Institute of Public Administration (IPA). Basically, the system is one of contractual research where the contractor is the Department of the Public Service. Without decrying the results of research carried out under this system, I maintain that the procedure adopted in relation to the ESRI should be applied to the IPA. Under this arrangement, the initiative and final decision in regard to the topics selected for research lies with the user of the funds, not with their provider.

CONCLUSION

Against a background of renewed political commitment to administrative reform (a commitment not yet matched by action) this paper examines some of the implications of the sheer size of the public sector — a size which, while making reform all the more necessary, has made it even more difficult. Reform has not been helped by electorate cynicism and disillusionment which mounted as the gap between promise and achievement widened. The growth and complexity of the public sector have a number of implications for parliamentary democracy. They have widened the gap between government and the governed. Long established conventions, such as ministerial responsibility for all departmental actions, have become untenable and implausible. The time required by ministers and governments to change entrenched economic and social trends has increased significantly. To redress the balance between politician and administrator, should politics become a full-time career and should we pay our politicians accordingly? Growth has been accompanied by a search for consensus, but in most cases the demands made on the time and effort of the community have not yet been justified by the results. Growth has, unfortunately, not been accompanied by the independent administrative research required to draw the correct lessons from past mistakes, to identify the most promising areas for cost reductions, and to provide the basis for objective, critical appraisal of the public sector.

4

The Mystery of Government: Civil Servants and Politics

This article first appeared in IBAR — Journal of Irish Business and Administrative Research, *Vol. 7, No. 1, 1985*

In a striking phrase, a British politician has referred to 'the mystery of government — namely how an apolitical civil service can truly serve a very political minister' (Williams, 1982). This is a mystery which Ireland shares with Britain, if not, indeed, with others. My purpose in this article is not to solve the mystery, but rather to explore some of its implications for Ministers, the civil service and, not least, for democracy. Given the limitations of space, the emphasis will be on four aspects: Civil Servants and Politics; Civil Servants and Policy Formulation; Civil Servants and Ministers; and Civil Servants and Parliamentary Democracy. These divisions are not watertight. It is easy to put a case in a nutshell, but not so easy to keep it there.

CIVIL SERVANTS AND POLITICS

My starting point is the widely accepted concept of the political impartiality of the civil service. Whether this places the civil service above, below, or beyond politics is a matter of semantics. This impartiality is intended to ensure not alone the continuity of public administration irrespective of changes in government, but also a willingness to work *for* the government of the day and *against* the government of yesterday. Impartiality, in other words, is not neutrality. It has been described as a chameleon-like ability to identify with successive governments of quite different political complexions (Ridley, 1983).

It is easy to count the advantages of such a system. The disadvantages are often overlooked. Commitment and impartiality are uneasy bedfellows. A civil servant can be relied upon to implement policies with which he profoundly disagrees, but will he regard the task as an ardent obligation, and will his commitment be more than formal? The system takes a lot for granted. As one British observer has forcefully put it:

> British administrative practice ... works on the assumption ... that people of ability, of power, and influence, in the higher civil service can feel no sense of impropriety, futility, dishonesty or disloyalty, either to the state or to their party (if they have one) or to their consciences, by working as hard as they can to execute the policy of one party and defend it against the Opposition, and then reverse the roles completely when the Opposition becomes the govenment (Rose, 1969).

Even with goodwill, impartiality can come under strain. As I pointed out in an earlier article:

> Commitment and dedication can suffer if there are abrupt and frequent reversals of policy; in administration, as in parliamentary democracy, there has to be respect for, and observation of, a minimum level of agreed conventions. Strain can also result from other factors. Thus a political utterance clearly at variance with facts known to the civil servant may not put his or her loyalty or silence at risk, but it can make civil servants sceptical of the political process (Chapter 2, 'A Working and Changeable Instrument').

We have accepted without much question the tradition of political impartiality of the civil service which we inherited from Britain, a tradition which is admirably summarised in the following words from a recently retired Permanent Secretary to the Treasury:

> The line which separates the politically committed and

publicly responsible Minister from the neutral permanent official is drawn at a particularly high level in Britain. In practically no other country is there so little change in the administrative apparatus when a government takes office (Wass, 1983).

This is not to suggest that we go to the opposite extreme of a spoils system. It is, however, salutary to remind ourselves that in other countries the divide between the civil service and politics is not quite so clearcut and absolute as it is here.

I am not aware of any comprehensive analysis of the European practice in this respect, but from the limited information available I am struck by the marked contrast between the Irish (and British) conventions, and those which obtain elsewhere in Europe.[31] In *Government and Administation in Western Europe* (Ridley, 1979) we learn that:

In France, 'most civil servants are allowed to join political parties and participate in their activities; they obtain leave to fight elections and, if elected, to serve in parliament' (p. 97);

In Germany, 'from B7 (undersecretary) all civil servants are "political" i.e. they can be pensioned off at the Minister's discretion. In filling such posts, Ministers may appoint someone from outside the department who may not necessarily have the ordinary civil service qualifications — about one third of appointees to these positions are outsiders' (p. 141);

'In Germany, civil servants and politicians are overlapping, not exclusive, categories' (p. 147).

In Belgium 'It is widely acknowledged that the (civil) service is highly politicised, that appointments and promotions are partly determined by political affiliation and that the behaviour of civil servants is influenced by their partisan preferences' (p. 221).

In the Netherlands 'Ministers may not sit in Parliament and ... there is a strong tradition that Ministers should be specialists in the work of their ministry. This often means that they are actually civil servants from within the Ministry ...' (pp. 229-30).

Other sources confirm these statements. We learn that:

In France 'it has become difficult to draw a clear distinction between administrative and political posts — the distinction has in any case become somewhat academic because civil servants are now appointed to what are really political posts, previously held by Parliamentarians only' (Open University Press, 1982).

In Germany 'it is accepted that certain jobs in the civil service, especially at senior levels, are liable — and likely — to change with administrations' (Neville-Jones, 1983).

The civil servant/politician is not confined to continental Europe. In Japan 'The civil service head of a Japanese Department is a Vice-Minister and he generally goes on to become head of a business or full Minister. Many Japanese Prime Ministers have been former civil servants' (Pliatzky, 1984).

Public administration in the United States of America is popularly identified with the spoils system but, given the complexity and scale of the public sector, it is not surprising that the spoils are contained, to some extent, within the civil service: 'One-third to one-half of the 600 non-career supergrade posts and anywhere from one-fifth to two-fifths of the higher political appointments are usually filled by career civil servants' (Heclo, 1977).

There is, of course, one way in which politics *could* leave its imprint on the Irish civil service. Recruitment is removed from political patronage by being channelled through the Civil Service Commission. Promotion at the top is a matter for ministers and — in the case of departmental secretaries — for the government. I readily acknowledge that, with one or two doubtful exceptions over a long period, I am not aware of any senior appointments which were due to political influence. Whether this is a testimony to the system, or a reflection of my naïveté, I leave it to others to judge. The Minister for the Public Service has introduced (incidentally, without consultation with staff) some major changes in the system of senior promotions in the civil service. It is to be hoped that the new system will maintain the long standing tradition of political neutrality in these matters. Let us take warning from the doubts being expressed in Britain of Mrs. Thatcher's active involvement in senior promotions there. As one commentator put it:

> Intervention by politicians in promotion, even if it does not have a straight party political character, tends to

politicise the civil service and thus calls into question the constitutional convention that senior officials are the neutral servants of successive governments' (Ridley, 1983).

The discussion so far has centred on some aspects of the relationship between the civil service and politics. Others would see this relationship in quite a different light. For them, civil servants are policy makers and are, therefore, engaged in politics. Let me now turn to this argument.

CIVIL SERVANTS AND POLICY FORMULATION

I sometimes think that the old scholastic disputation about the number of angels who could fit on the point of a needle is a disputation about reality compared with the argument about the role of the civil servant in the formulation of public policy. It is no help to be reminded that a British observer has dismissed the difference between 'politics' and 'policy' as 'verbal hypocrisy' (Chapman, 1963). There is, of course, no difficulty in rejecting the argument at either extreme — for example, that civil servants have no function whatsoever in regard to policy or, alternatively, that ministers have only formal, but no real, functions in regard to such decisions. The problem is to locate where precisely, or even approximately, between these two extremes the truth is to be found. An easy answer is to say that everything depends on the specific case being considered and that the answer will change over time and with the circumstances and personalities involved. True enough — but one must still search for some general principles, however weak and shortlived. The late Sean Lemass formulated such a principle in an interview published in 1968:

> The end product of every investigation or study carried out in a Government Department should be a Ministerial or Government decision. I think it was John Fitzgerald Kennedy who said that a function of the Civil Service expert was to examine a question to a conclusion, while the function of the political head of his Department was to examine it to a decision. Whether in the formulation of

new policies or the fulfilment of older ones, the mainspring of activity in every Department of Government is the Ministerial decision. On the Minister's capacity to give speedy and clear decisions on matters coming up to him from the Department and also the extent to which the understanding of the Minister's aims permeates all its activities depends the effectiveness of every Department. In the same way, new ideas emerging from Departmental studies make no progress until the Minister gives them his endorsement and support (Lemass, 1968).

I suspect that this formulation owes much to Mr. Lemass's forceful personality and his commitment to action. An American study suggests four competing theories to explain what is at issue:

Theory I:
Politicians make policy; civil servants administer.

Theory II:
Both politicians and civil servants participate in making policy — civil servants bring facts and knowledge; politicians, interests and values. Civil servants bring neutral expertise — will it work? — while politicians bring political sensitivity — will it fly?

Theory III:
Both bureaucrats and politicians engage in policy making, and both are concerned with politics. The real distinction between them is this; whereas politicians articulate broad, diffuse interests of unorganised individuals, bureaucrats mediate narrow, focused interests of organised clienteles. In this interpretation of the division of labour, politicians are passionate, partisan, idealistic, even ideological; bureaucrats are, by contrast, prudent, centrist, practical, pragmatic. Politicians seek publicity, raise innovative issues, are energising to the policy system, whereas bureaucrats prefer the back room, manage incremental adjustments, and provide policy equilibrium (per Webster's 'a state of balance between opposing forces or actions').

Theory IV:
Suggests speculatively that the last quarter of this century is witnessing the virtual disappearance of the Weberian distinction between the roles of politician and bureaucrat, producing what we might label a 'pure hybrid':

> . . . . the notion that in behavioural terms the two roles have been converging — perhaps reflecting, as some have argued, a 'politicisation' of the bureaucracy and a 'bureaucratisation' of politics. (Aberbach, Putnam, Rockman, 1981).

I can well understand the puzzlement and frustration of the public at statements such as this. Whom, they want to know, are we to blame, or, perhaps very occasionally, to thank? Where do we find the seat of power? If policies should be changed, who is responsible for making the change? I can offer only a personal, tentative, and, doubtless, biased answer. In our system of parliamentary democracy I see the responsibility for policies lying primarily with ministers, not alone in a formal, legal sense, but also in a practical sense. Civil servants, however, have their own responsibilities. They cannot adopt a passive role, content to operate existing policies without regard to their continuing validity or relevance, refusing to consider whether changes are required by changing circumstances. They have a responsibility to advise ministers on the need for change and to press this advice as forcefully as they can. They can do no more. In this they resemble the ancient Netherlands Order of the Golden Fleece, a company whose duty it was to give advice to the Dutch ruler to be backed by solemn oath to speak freely, honestly, and under privilege.

This is not an original or even a particularly useful way of explaining the complicated relationship between civil servants and politicians. It certainly will not please those who see in the civil service the real or permanent government of the country, who regard civil servants as possessing, in Stanley Baldwin's phrase regarding the press, power without responsibility — the prerogative of the harlot throughout the ages. It is a far cry — at the other extreme — from Lenin's boast that: 'We will reduce the role of State officials to that of simply carrying out our instructions as responsible, revocable, modestly paid foremen and accountants' (McLellan, 1983).

The more interesting question is whether civil servants do, in fact, discharge the limited, though important, responsibility I have mentioned. Not all would be willing to award a pass mark to the civil service on this question, or even to give it E for effort. Have they, however, ever stopped to ask themselves why people, whose commitment and ability are not in question, may fail in this important respect? I myself have no doubts where the fault lies. The sheer pressure of detail on Ministers and senior civil servants has prevented both from developing that most useful of attributes — clear vision over long distances. Only those who work at, or close to, the centre, can have any idea of the maelstrom in the middle. The Devlin Review Committee, which reported as long as sixteen years ago, sought the remedy in the concentration of policy-making in small ministerial units called Aireachts, while the execution of policy would be entrusted to executive units for which ministers would have no day-to-day responsibility. This recommendation has not yet been implemented. The to-ing and fro-ing on this issue reminds me of the man with a headache who convinces himself that by combing his hair he is getting close to the problem, failing to recognise that he is as far away as ever from a solution.

CIVIL SERVANTS AND MINISTERS

Everything done by a department is done in the name of the minister who is legally and politically responsible for its acts and omissions. Carried to its logical conclusion, this doctrine would bring all public sector business to a virtual standstill. Only a massive system of delegation makes sense of this legal fiction. I stress the fictional aspect of this responsibility because very few, if any, ministers have, in fact resigned because of it in over sixty years of self government. But a price has had to be paid. Much of the criticism of the civil service stems from procedures and practices derived from the outdated and irrelevant concept of ministerial responsibility. I say this, not to absolve the civil service from all responsibility. Their responsibility — as it was mine when I was a civil servant — is to devise and press for a workable alternative rather than passively accept the defects of the present system. The public is getting the worst of both worlds — a system unnecessarily complicated and inflexible because of the doctrine of ministerial responsibility, yet one which lacks the drive and punch which full acceptance of ministerial responsibility would ensure.

An unsatisfactory feature of the present system is the difficulty of apportioning blame when things go wrong. I have in mind not so much executive errors as policy mistakes. Some ministers are inclined to blame the pianist, not his score, when the music does not please. Stronger ministers are, of course, in no doubt where the buck stops. Let me quote Sean Lemass once again:

> The effective Minister is one who gives all proper weight to the advice and options of his top officials but who, nevertheless, takes his own decisions, in accordance with the policy of his Government, and thereafter ensures that his decisions are fully carried out. Ministers who are considered by the public and their political associates to be competent and effective Ministers are those who remain in full control of their Departments in all aspects of policy making.

The late Richard Crossman was equally definite:

> . . . it is our (politicians') job to have creative ideas and bring them in. What's a (political) party for except to be the vehicle for creative change? That's our function — to provide the catalyst in Whitehall — and also the instrument of change. Why should I expect the civil service to do it? . . . I am not surprised not many creative ideas come out of the British Civil Service. Nor do I blame the civil servants for this (Crossman, 1972).

William Rodgers, a former British Minister, was no less emphatic:

> The last resort of an incompetent minister is to blame his civil servants. The last resort of a government that has failed

is to make the Civil Service, as a whole, the scapegoat (Rodgers, 1982).

THE CIVIL SERVICE AND PARLIAMENTARY DEMOCRACY

The massive increase in the size of the public sector, the extension of its frontiers, the many demands on a minister's time, apart from running his department, and many other factors have serious implications for parliamentary democracy. They have led to frustration and remoteness, indeed alienation, between those who govern and those who are governed. In the vivid imagery of Tom Barrington (1982): 'It is as if an ice floe were to crack and break, leaving government on the one part and governed on the other, each drifting steadily, inexorably apart.'

The growth in the size of the public sector has blurred the difference in functions between civil servants and politicians in regard to policy formulation. It has tilted the balance of power between the two, and tilted it to the detriment of the politician. It has extended the time required not alone to prepare a comprehensive economic and social plan, but also to test and validate the plan in practice. Time is further extended by what I can only call the passion for consultation and the search for consensus, where diminishing returns have long since set in. I am most familiar with the phenomenon in the economic sphere in organisations such as the Committee on Industrial Organisation, the National Industries and Economic Council and the National Economic and Social Council. I would guess that NESC is approaching the two million word mark — if only words alone were enough!*

The factors I have mentioned put a premium on long-life governments and underline the problem created by recent short-lived governments. The life of a government has been described as comprising three periods — those of euphoria, remorse, and preparation for the next election. Recent governments have telescoped the three periods into one. It is

---

*But see footnote, page 55.

easy to forget that in the last five years we have had five Ministers for Finance and that, in the same period, only two ministers have brought in more than one budget. We have had seven Transport Ministers in the last ten years or so. What price fiscal and transport policies?

In some countries, though not so far in Ireland, these developments have led commentators to urge that civil servants should see themselves as more than servants of the government of the day. Civil servants, on this argument, should balance their responsibility to transient politicians with a responsibility for the permanent interests of the country. This is a sophisticated gloss on the old argument which exalted civil servants at the expense of ministers who were dismissed as birds of passage. I am sceptical, indeed afraid, of this line of argument. I leave aside such difficulties as how to identify the permanent interests of the country and how to serve them rather than the policies favoured by the government of the day. My opposition stems rather from democratic principles. If the government policies are faulty, the electorate, not the civil servant, should attempt to replace them by other policies. Whatever functions the civil service has in regard to policy formulation — and I have made it clear that its role is not passive — they do not extend to substituting its own judgement and decision for those of the electorate. To proceed otherwise, even assuming it were possible, would be to make a mockery of parliamentary democracy.

I accept that things may be ordered differently elsewhere. In France for example, civil servants 'have traditionally seen themselves as servants of the state, serving a national interest they define themselves, rather than the simple instruments of party politicians' (Ridley, 1979). And in Germany 'The Civil Service Law of 1953 incorporated the requirement that the civil servant should be an active defender of the democratic order. Civil servants regarded themselves as a supplementary source of leadership to party politicians because they were servants of the state which stands above politics' (Southern, 1979).

It is wise, however, to bear in mind that this is not the only way in which civil service traditions and practices elsewhere differ from those in Ireland. The approach elsewhere to the wider responsibilities of civil servants has to be seen in the context of attitudes elsewhere to civil servants and politics, to which I referred earlier. If a similar approach were to be adopted in this country, it could not simply be superimposed on the existing system. Other rules of the game would perforce be changed; it would remain to be seen whether, on balance, the national interest would best be served.

Let me emphasise, however, that I appreciate, while not wholly accepting, the viewpoint of those who contend that, under the present system, the responsibilities of the civil service are vague and often unenforceable. My contention is simply that the answer does not lie in making the service answerable to some ill-defined concept such as the public interest.

CONCLUSION

My aim in this article has been to show how the civil service relates to politics, or, as I would prefer to put it, how it fits into the system of government. I have tried to show that many simple statements about this relationship are just that — simple. Indeed, if I had to choose one word to describe the relationship, it would be ambiguous.

The Minister for the Public Service has announced that a White Paper will be published on civil service reform. One of his suggestions, if adopted in the spirit as well as in the letter, could have far reaching results. He has suggested the abolition of the concept of the minister as a corporation sole, the concept which is the legal basis of ministerial responsibility. Past experience leads me to doubt whether politicians will readily relinquish their hold on the reins which control the public service. To abolish legal constraints is one thing, to relinquish political power is another. This reluctance may reflect, in part, pressure from the electorate and the politicians' need for re-election, a pressure and a need all the greater in our system of proportional representation.

Tadhg O'Cearbhaill, former Secretary of the Department of Labour, has shrewdly pointed out that:

. . . there is one reality which will have to be recognised. It is that the public, and particular sections of it who may feel aggrieved from time to time, are acutely aware of their elected Parliamentary representative and they expect him to advance as best he can the interests of those who elected him. Any Civil Service reform that fails to take account of that reality cannot be expected to endure (1982).

It is an intriguing thought that the remedy — or the beginning of the remedy — for the problems of the civil service may lie in the hands of the electorate.

5

Serving the Country Better: Comments on the White Paper

This article first appeared in Seirbhís Phoiblí *Vol. 6, No. 4, 1985*

This is a unique White Paper. In our sixty-three years of independence, it is the first formal Government document on the public service, in general, and on the civil service, in particular. It is idle to speculate on the reasons for this long gestation period. Suffice it to say that the White Paper is long overdue.

Ironically, when it did appear, its broad thrust, and much of its detail, did not come as a surprise. This was because its way had been made smooth by many Ministerial pronouncements and also by the Government's Plan, *Building on Reality*. These had alerted the public to what the White Paper itself states is at the centre of the Government's plans for tomorrow's public service, namely 'a management improvement programme which will involve the introduction in all departments of management systems based on corporate planning and emphasising personal responsibility for results, costs and services (paragraph 1.14). Much of the White Paper is devoted to crossing the t's and dotting the i's of this New Deal which will sound the death-knell of the Circumlocution Office satirised by Dickens, an office which 'was beforehand with all the public departments in the art of perceiving — HOW NOT TO DO IT'.

In its insistent stress on management and the personal responsibility of civil servants for an efficient service, the White Paper mercifully avoids the usual facile and misleading analogies with the private sector. It recognises — although perhaps not fully — that the existing system must be changed in other respects if the objective of an efficient and accountable system of management is to be achieved and sustained. Chief among these changes is the establishment of executive offices whose chief executives 'will be given greater managerial autonomy than is normally possible within the civil service context, including authority in relation to appointment, discipline and dismissal of staff . . .' (paragraph 3:10). Executive offices will be established where there is a 'sufficiently large volume of purely executive work' (paragraph 3.9), and the work transferred to them 'will no longer be regarded as part of the business of the department for which the Minister is responsible' (paragraph 3.10).

Fair enough — but is not all this reminiscent of the Devlin Report which, sixteen years ago, recommended the establishment of Aireachts, Executive Offices, and Executive Units? That recommendation was accepted *in principle* by successive Governments and was put into effect on a trial basis in a significant number of departments. There does not exist — to my knowledge — an account of this experiment and an assessment of the results achieved. It is disturbing to find that the White Paper does not acknowledge the provenance of its central recommendation, still less tell us what lessons can be learned from these earlier experiments. There is, of course, one formal difference between the Aireacht experiments and what is now proposed. During the currency of the Aireacht experiments, the Ministers concerned were still formally responsible for what was done or not done in their departments, but this hardly vitiates the point I am making.

The White Paper recognises that more positive action is required if executive offices are to be managed efficiently and effectively. It rightly places the emphasis on people rather than structures. Promotion procedures are being changed; I will touch on these later. The fact that the chief executives of the executive offices will have *full responsibility* should help to concentrate their minds. They will be responsible for their own budgets and will have certain powers to appoint and dismiss staff and to offer merit pay. A judgement on how effective these powers will be must be deferred until more details become available. Let us hope that excess and frustrating uniformity — for example in regard to merit pay — will be avoided.

While I welcome the central proposal of the White Paper, I am under no illusion about the difficulties involved. My reservations do not arise from the theoretical argument that a Minister's formal responsibility should not be diluted in any way, or that it is wrong to drive a wedge between the work of advising on policy and the work of policy execution. I would shed no tears for the death of the concept of comprehensive ministerial responsibility and the replacement of the present legal fiction by a more realistic concept. As regards the policy versus execution issue, I suggest that there are quite enough clear-cut, unambiguous, examples of executive work to enable the proposal to be put into widespread effect.

EXECUTIVE OFFICES: SOME RESERVATIONS

Before I outline my main reservations, let me point to one aspect which concerns me. The proposal is that all departments will have management systems based on *personal* responsibility for results and value for money (paragraphs 1.14 and 2.5). The position should be clear-cut, formally at least, where executive offices are established. But what about those blocks of work not large enough 'to make it feasible to set up separate organisations for (their) performance' (paragraph 3.9)?

In such cases, since the Minister's formal responsibility remains, the managers concerned cannot be assigned *full* responsibility for the efficient discharge of the work, and in such cases a central feature of the new scheme will be lacking — unless the existing legislation is amended.

Turning now to my main reservations (which let me repeat, apply not to the principle, but rather to the application, of managerial responsibility in the civil service) these fall under a number of headings:

- Cost-effectiveness must be based on a medium-term plan covering at least three years and preferably not less than five years. In a public sector context, this means that there must be a reasonably firm commitment regarding current and capital expenditure targets for the plan period. On past experience there is little ground for confidence that this requirement will be met. The record of the present Government is somewhat more reassuring, but it is too soon yet to be certain that departments and executive offices will have the assurance of (and be confined to) specific funds for three or five years ahead, subject always, of course, to a minimum tolerance in either direction and to unavoidable adjustments resulting from major unforeseen developments. In the absence of such an assurance, managerial performance must inevitably be subject to a greater or lesser element of *ad hocery* — particularly if Governments are short lived.

● The responsibility of *all* departments to introduce management systems based on personal responsibility for results and value for money presupposes that all results can be quantified with reasonable certainty. The White Paper rather disarmingly recognises the problem in this respect:

'It is accepted that many civil service "outputs" do not readily lend themselves to quantification and that the evaluation of their effectiveness is often subjective. . . .' (paragraph 2.12).

I accept that a start must be made; and that it would be stultifying to allow the better to be the enemy of the good. Nevertheless, this point is so crucial to the central theme of the report that I would have expected a fuller and more realistic treatment of it.

● Cost effectiveness can be achieved by minimising inputs or maximising outputs, or by a combination of each. Given the difficulty in many cases of defining and identifying outputs, the tendency could develop of laying *undue* stress on minimising inputs. This could well result in a more 'efficient' use of resources but not necessarily in a more efficient way of achieving the maximum sustainable increase in public well-being — leading in the extreme, as an English commentator has put it, to a new Wildean culture of management which knows the costs of everything but the value of nothing (Gray and Jenkins, 1984).

● Even in the New Deal, civil service managers will operate under restrictions without parallel in the private sector. Their right to hire and fire will be circumscribed and they will have to take pay policy as given. They will — apparently — have no say in the engagement and placement of the one thousand trainees proposed in the White Paper, a proposal which, however laudable, will hardly enhance efficiency. More significantly, they will be faced with the heavy — and often frustrating — duty of satisfying the many Oireachtas Committees concerned, directly or indirectly, with public expenditure. I note with alarm that yet another such committee (admittedly a child of two existing ones) is to be established. I suggest that a cost-benefit study should be made of this rash of committees; some benefits may be undeniable, but do they fully justify the costs?

● The formal management systems which will underpin the New Deal comprise two complementary elements. One is financial management, already initiated by the Department of Finance. The other is a total management system, to be initiated by the Department of the Public Service. The White Paper emphasises that the Government 'does not envisage two separate systems being developed side by side in each department, and stresses that the two central departments 'will coordinate their approach to departments about these matters' (paragraph 2.11). Despite these protestations, the suspicion must remain that problems will be caused by overlap and duplication, not alone for the central departments, but also for the line departments. While these can be minimised by inter-departmental coordination, is the net effect the most effective way of implementing the White Paper?[32]

Despite these reservations, I consider that the Government was fully justified in making efficiency the central theme of the White Paper. The public is entitled to maximum efficiency from the civil service — but efficiency has to be defined in a public service context and measured (where measurement is possible) by a public service yardstick.

INSTITUTIONAL CHANGES NOT ENOUGH

Productivity is achieved by people, not by institutions or by institutional change. The White Paper acknowledges that changes in personnel practices are required if 'personal responsibility for results, costs and services' is to become more effective. It is possible that it under-estimates the changes required, since morale in the service may not be very high at present. A variety of factors, such as widespread, indiscriminate criticisms, dingy offices, the infamous embargo, confrontations over pay, do not provide a propitious background for the encouragement of initiative and of motivation without which the structural changes will not be effective. I do not doubt the inherent ability of the civil service to overcome the profound culture-shock involved but it would be unwise to ignore the extent to which it may have been conditioned by the *mores* of the present system; to adapt Lloyd George's phrase about Asquith, civil servants have sat on the fence so long that the iron may have entered their souls. There may also be generational gap problems; I hope that there will be special consideration for any older officers who may find it particularly difficult to enter the Brave New World of the New Deal.

The impression is subtly conveyed that the New Deal will break entirely new ground in ensuring that merit will be the over-riding consideration in promotions. The formal position hitherto has been that the promotee must be not alone fully qualified for the job, but also the best qualified of all the eligible officers. Taking the civil service as a whole, it could well be that seniority has been given an undue weight in applying this criterion, but this would not be true of all Departments and certainly not true of promotions to the most senior posts. I think that it would be fairer to say that the New Deal will give — or, rather, proposes to give — much greater weight to merit and much less to seniority, particularly at junior and middle levels; it undoubtedly envisages a vast increase in interdepartmental mobility. All this will involve a great deal of added work, not alone in identifying merit but also in demonstrating to the unsuccessful that procedures are fair and impartial; it is a far cry from Duncan's pathetic belief that 'There is no art to find the mind's construction in the face'. I hope that, despite the army of interviewers engaged in assessing the merit of all grades from Clerical Assistants to Secretaries as they move from department to department, there will be enough time left over to get on with the real work. I hope, too, that a reasonable balance will be struck between merit and experience; if experience is ignored or diminished unduly, the net effect on *total* staff morale could well be negative.

There will be no regrets at the termination of the 'one-in-three' embargo, the only surprise being that it has taken so long to end such an unsatisfactory system. While it had the merit of working, after a fashion, it was no substitute for *selective* staff reductions based on a critical assessment of work loads and staff needs. All the more disappointing then, to find the White Paper so vague on what is to take its place. As an interim measure i.e. to end 1987, 'appropriate staffing levels' are to be fixed for each department, a year hence, as will be the proportion of vacancies arising during the year which may be filled by each department. Work on this matter must surely be far advanced, and the White Paper might have earned more conviction if it had presented the results. If work is not far advanced, can the interim measure be made operational in the short period allotted to it? By the end of the period of the National Plan (i.e. 1987) departments will be allowed to decide their staffing, subject to predetermined staffing budgets (paragraph 8.10). What exactly is meant by this important qualification?

The proposed abolition of the 'dual structure' and the progressive simplification of the grading structure bring back memories of the Devlin Report and contribute to the impression of *déjà vu*. The White Paper ignores Devlin, and, of course, bypasses in silence the lack of progress with the Devlin recomendations on these issues.

TOP LEVEL APPOINTMENTS

The Top Level Appointments system, introduced in January

1984, has produced some interesting results. By September 1985, 36 posts had been filled in this way. About 30% of these involved promotion across departmental boundaries. Somewhat surprisingly the proportion rose to 50% in the case of promotion to Secretary, and fell to 27% in the (more numerous) case of promotions to Assistant Secretary (including one promotion to Deputy Secretary). It is significant that (with one exception which is more apparent than real) promotions to fill vacancies in departmental grades did *not* involve any crossover from general service to departmental grades. Nor has there been any over-leaping of grades from Principal Officer to Secretary. It could be argued that the inter-departmental element in the new promotion system should not have extended, initially, to promotions to Secretary, given the more exacting nature of the responsibilities, and the need to have a good grasp of all Departmental policies and activities; when the new system, modified as suggested, had been in operation for some time, it could then be extended to cover promotions to Secretary.

The Top Level Appointments Committee is free to recommend that a post can be filled by way of a competition open to persons not already in the civil service. It is not known whether the Committee made any such recommendation which was rejected by the Government. What is known is that, to date, no post has been filled in this way.

When the new appointments system was introduced, it was stated that Departmental Secretaries would in future be appointed only for a seven year term — a recognition of the pressures at the top and the need to make way for new thinking. I certainly would not reject the principle involved, as I made a somewhat similar recommendation ten years or so ago. While accepting the principle of a restricted period of service at the top, one can have reservations about the appropriate length of that service — but seven years seems about right. When the scheme was introduced, no mention was made of what was to happen to a Secretary on the expiration of his or her seven year period of office, at a time when he or she might have many years of service to go before optional retirement (at 60 years) or compulsory retirement (at 65 years); in some cases the time involved could be 15-20 years. Was the *functus officius* to be

retired to the ranks, as happens in some monastic orders? Was
some state-sponsored body to be given the benefit of his or
her services — provided a suitable niche could be found? It
is disappointing to find that this matter is not mentioned, still
less resolved, in the White Paper.

There is a related matter — early retirement — which will
assume greater importance in the New Deal. Efficiency could
well be improved, and some personal distress solved, if senior
officers were given the opportunity of early retirement on less
austere terms than those at present available. The other side
of this coin is the availability of sabbatical leave for middle
grades upwards. A recent and welcome development has been
the career break scheme under which civil servants can take
special leave without pay for a period of not less than one year
and not more than three years; in the short period since its
introduction, over 1,000 have applied, truly a remarkable
figure. I have in mind a scheme at once more limited and more
generous, designed to provide officers at mid-career upwards
with an opportunity to study some aspects of their work, and
to return to the service, refreshed and, hopefully, revitalised.
The numbers involved at any one time would be quite small
(a dozen or so), the period would not exceed one year, but the
special leave would be *with pay*. Many details would have to
be worked out, many objections overcome — but a
Government committed to an efficient, innovative civil service
should not find this modest suggestion too difficult to handle.
The T.K. Whitaker Research Fellowship tenable at the
Economic and Social Research Institute could provide a
precedent.

While civil servants, up to and including Clerical Officers,
will have contracts of employment with statutory rights under
labour legislation, all others will presumably continue to serve
'at the will and pleasure' of the Government. Hopefully the
legislation envisaged in the White Paper will put an end to this
archaic fiction.

SOME ISSUES NOT CONSIDERED

The White Paper is noteworthy not alone for its wide coverage but also for some important issues on which it does not touch. I have not in mind such important issues as changes in the way parliament and Government go about their work: while changes are needed, the present White Paper is not the place to discuss them. I have in mind issues that are more directly related to the work of the civil service. There is, for example, no reference whatsoever to official secrecy, no suggestion that this issue is even 'under consideration', still less a recognition that a civil service in which there is personal responsibility and greater accountability for results, costs, and services, may find that the Official Secrets Acts, as they stand at present, are unduly restrictive. As was pointed out in a recent issue of this journal, 'any proposal to devolve a relative degree of autonomy on individual civil servants comes directly into conflict with the absolute nature of Ministerial authority as defined under the existing Official Secrecy legislation. Logically, therefore, it would seem unwise for any civil servant to accept greater responsibility without commensurate authority, both *de facto* and *de jure*' (Cook, 1985). I am not suggesting that the legislation should be replaced by an Official Disclosure Act, but some easement is surely warranted — and might have the incidental effect of reducing the distressing number of leaks. Nor am I suggesting that this is the only reason why a change in the law should be considered.

The White Paper does not make any reference to a much-loved panacea of some critics of the civil service, namely the *cabinet* system. Ministers have, of course, an undeniable right to appoint extern advisers in their Departments. Many have done so, with benefit to the civil service. The Irish arrangements, however, fall far short of the Continental *cabinet* system. If there were to be any significant increase in the numbers of advisers, there would need to be a clearer understanding than at present about their role and how they could best be integrated with the permanent civil service. By its silence, the White Paper does not see any major contribution towards a better civil service coming from this direction.

The fact that the White Paper makes only a cursory reference to administrative research is surprising in view of the strong endorsement of the need for research in the report of the Committee for Administrative Research which was presented to the Minister for the Public Service in November 1984.[33] The Committee consists of representatives from the Department of the Public Service, the Institute of Public Administration, the Economic and Social Research Institute, University College Dublin and Trinity College Dublin. It endorsed the need for a programme of research 'closely aligned to the public service modernisation programme, reflecting the areas of concern to the programme'. It identified three priority research themes for the period 1985-1990 — management practices and behaviour, the administration and the citizen, and the changing work environment.[34]

The White Paper understandably concentrates on one of the two broad functions performed by the civil service, namely 'the delivery of a wide range of services to the public', and on ways by which these services might be delivered more efficiently and effectively. It recognises that the other broad function — 'the formulation of policy, advice and planning on behalf of the Government' is 'of the utmost importance if the challenges of the future are to be met' (paragraph 1.12). Beyond this recognition, the White Paper ignores this second function, although some of the issues discussed (e.g. the Top Level Appointments Committee) have a bearing on it. This treatment may reflect satisfaction with things as they are, or the difficulty of prescribing for such an ill-defined activity. Whatever the reason, the emphasis on management in the White Paper may inadvertently lead to an imbalance between the two functions and, consequently, to a diminution in the importance of Ministers in public administration.

Serving the Country Better is described as a White Paper on the Public Service. The description is somewhat of a misnomer. The document itself makes it clear that 'The emphasis. . .is largely, although not entirely, on the civil service' (paragraph 1.7). In fact little enough is said about the rest of the public service. Because of pressure of space, I will confine my comments to one issue — the controversial statement on pay policy in the commercial state-sponsored bodies. While respecting the need for managerial autonomy, it is proposed that 'the statutory requirement (which at present applies to some bodies) that the Board would abide by Government policies and have regard to any Government directives on pay and conditions of employment will be extended to all' (paragraph 8.14). This further encroachment on the commercial autonomy of these bodies brings nearer the day when their whole *raison d'être* must be seriously re-assessed.

A FIRM ACTION PLAN?

It is, perhaps, of the nature of comments such as these that attention is focused more on points of disagreement than of agreement, and that emphasis is laid on criticism rather than on approval. Let me make it clear, in these concluding remarks, that I welcome this White Paper both in its broad thrust and in most of its specific recommendations. But can we say that we have seen the future, and it works?

The White Paper describes itself 'as a statement of decisions taken and a firm action plan' (para. 9.1). It is easy to be cynical about the commitment of politicians and civil servants to take 'firm action' on administrative changes. Few of them can look to the past with pride. For reasons which do not necessarily reflect discredit on those concerned, previous administrative innovations have not lived up to their promises — or perhaps expectations were pitched too high. The past is littered with their acronyms — PPBS, MBO, CB, OR, ADP etc. It would, however, be wrong to write them off, and perhaps they will flourish in the more favourable climate provided by the New Deal.

The New Deal will suffer the fate of the Devlin Report unless there is a whole-hearted commitment from Ministers and civil servants. There will be obstacles. Some public servants will probably reject parts of the New Deal — such as the veiled suggestion that access to the Labour Court should be withdrawn from those public service groups which at present have that privilege; I hope that they will not reject the whole because they dislike the part. A pointer to the likely reaction of civil servants generally may be gleaned from the response to the establishment of the Ombudsman's Office. In his first report, the Ombudsman described the response of many civil servants as 'most encouraging' and stated that many of them 'cooperated whole-heartedly'. He did not, however, give the civil service a blank cheque of approval. Some senior civil servants 'had considerable suspicions about the new institution and resented its intrusion, particularly when their decisions were under scrutiny'.[35] Let this rebuke be a warning to the higher civil service; their commitment to the New Deal should be active rather than passive, real rather than formal — an ardent obligation, in short. The Government, for its part, must make the New Deal a cooperative enterprise with the civil service and must involve the service actively and positively in making it effective. Let there be no illusion about how difficult and longdrawn out the changeover will be. The New Deal will help, but will not solve, the critical state of the public finances, which, while providing a spur for reform, creates a most difficult environment for change.

There is a tendency — common to many Governments — of mistaking a cherished programme for an achieved reality.[36] Let me, therefore, apply, a simple, though not conclusive, test of the firmness of the action plan. The necessary legislation is to be introduced 'immediately' (paragraph 9). As the general lines of this legislation have been approved by the Government (paragraph 9.6), it should be possible to have it introduced, and, hopefully, enacted by the end of this year. Unless, of course, the Iron Law of Administration applies — it often takes longer than you think.

6

A Hundred Flowers of Criticism

Let a hundred flowers of criticism bloom — Mao Tse Tung

This article first appeared in Seirbhís Phoiblí, *Vol. 7, No. 3, 1986*

Over twenty years ago a senior English civil servant warned his colleagues 'that we shall continue to be grouped with mothers-in-law and Wigan Pier as one of the recognised subjects of ridicule' (Bridges, 1971).

What warning should be given to their Irish counterparts? Perhaps the question might be phrased more neutrally — how is the Irish civil service regarded by the public it serves?

One answer is provided by the Irish Report of the European Value Systems Study published under the title *Irish Values and Attitudes* (Fogarty, Ryan and Lee, Dominican Publications 1984). Table 18(b) in that study dealt with confidence in national institutions — by religion. The institutions covered were the Church, police, armed forces, education system, legal system, civil service, parliament, major companies, press and trade unions. The position regarding the civil service is shown in Table 1:

Table 1: Confidence in the civil service

	Percentage of each group				
	Catholic	Protestant	No religion	Convinced Atheist	Weekly church attender
Confidence in Civil Service:					
– great deal	14	10	0	0	15
– quite a lot	41	32	18	21	44
– not very much/none	44	59	82	80	39

It would be interesting to know why confidence in the civil service is markedly less among Protestants, non-religionists and convinced atheists than among Catholics. What message should this have for the civil service? Before we read too much into these variations, it is well to note that, by and large, the pattern is the same in regard to the other institutions — so that any questions about the differences between Catholics and others regarding confidence in the civil service must be tackled on a broader front.

It is not possible to derive national averages from this report but if, given the preponderance of Catholics in the population of the State, the figures relating to Catholics were taken as a proxy for those applicable to the State as a whole, it could be stated that 55% of the population had a great deal/quite a lot of confidence in the civil service.

Adopting the same approach in regard to the other institutions, the confidence factors compare as follows:

- Police   87
- The Church   79
- Armed Forces   76
- Education System   67
- Legal System   58
- Civil Service   55
- Parliament   53
- Major Companies   50
- Press   45
- Trade Unions   38

These figures should be read with caution; in particular, since they contain different mixes of the two confidence factors (great deal/quite a lot), inter-institutional comparisons should be treated with considerable reserve. The most that can be said is that the civil service, appropriately enough, occupies a middle-of-the-road position in the pecking order of confidence. Hardly a matter of self-congratulation, but certainly not one for self-flagellation.

MEANING OF CONFIDENCE

What do people mean when they say that they have no (or little) confidence in an organisation? The question has, I suggest, particular relevance in regard to the civil service (and other public sector institutions) whose *raison d'être* is service to the public. The term may, for example, convey that one holds the organisation in low esteem because it is inefficient or cannot be relied on to do the job it is supposed to do. In a civil service context the phrase could in addition convey the impression that the public considered that the civil service was not sufficiently zealous in serving the public interest, or was not impartial, or was corrupt. It is a pity that the European Value Systems Study, having indirectly raised questions such as these, fails to provide answers.

I wonder, indeed, whether confidence in the civil service has precisely the same meaning as it has in relation to the other institutions? For example, were those who answered the question clear about the distinction between, on the one hand, the kind of work discharged by the civil service and, on the other, the way in which they discharged this work? For many citizens, the civil service is seen as the purveyor of inadequate benefits (or, even, as the withholder of entitlements) or as the instrument for exacting (exorbitant) taxes. The fact that, in such cases, the civil service is the agent for executing Government policy is not always perceived by the citizens or, if it is, frustration at Government policies may be directed at the agent rather than at the principal.

POLITICAL CULTURE AND THE CIVIL SERVICE

To raise this point runs the risk of seeming complacent, of conveying the impression that a confidence rating is almost an irrelevant issue as far as the civil service is concerned. That certainly is not my intention. But I remain convinced that in assessing the confidence rating of the civil service, account must be taken of the political culture in which it operates. Most commentators agree that the dominating feature of that culture in Ireland is clientelism.[37] I am not aware of any discussion of the implications of clientelism for the role of the civil service and the regard in which it is held by the public. A survey of political culture in Ireland carried out in the early 1970's dealt only incidentally with this issue. Asked to rank different ways of influencing a Government decision, only 11% of the survey rated writing to government officials as the most effective way, while 30% rated such an approach as the least effective way. The authors commented that: 'Thus, although the question of confidence in appointed officials remains an open one, it is clear that they are not considered to be particularly influential figures in the legislative system' (Raven *et. al.*, 1976).

OMBUDSMAN'S REPORTS

The Ombudsman's reports should, over time, provide a useful insight into the relationship between the civil service and the public it serves. If complaints are taken as a proxy for lack of confidence, it is interesting to note how this lack of confidence is concentrated in a few departments, as Table 2, derived from the Ombudsman's Reports, indicates:

Table 2: **Complaints against departments**

	1984	*% of total*	*1985*	*% of total*
Social Welfare	744	55.0	1,383	57.6
Revenue Commissioners	295	21.8	424	17.9
Education	70	5.2	70	3.0
Environment	67	5.0	137	5.7
Agriculture	54	4.0	82	3.4
Other	122*	9.0	296	12.4
Total	1,352	100.0	2,392	100.0

*Excludes complaints (192) in relation to Posts and Telegraphs; the figures relating to An Bord Telecom are, of course, not included in the 1985 figure.

The Department of Social Welfare comes out somewhat better from this table than from a survey carried out in 1981 of the complaints handled by TDs: 'Within the civil service 84% of the deputies indicated the Department of Social Welfare as the department most frequently mentioned in complaints' (Roche, 1982).

A table in the first report of the Ombudsman suggests that the number of complaints he received in his first year of office (1984) was high relative to those received by his counterparts in other comparable countries. The table was not reproduced in the second report. It is, of course, too early to draw any firm international comparisons of this kind.

When account is taken of cases discontinued, withdrawn or not upheld, quite a number of departments and offices had a clean (or virtually clean) bill of administrative health in the two years covered by the Ombudsman's reports. The sceptic would say that this record may change in time as the public becomes more aware of the remedies available to them through the Office of the Ombudsman and, in any event, may reflect the extent to which the work of the institutions in question does not impinge on the vast bulk of the public. Fair enough, but it is salutary to bear in mind that this is yet another example of the fact that the civil service is not a monolith, that in some senses there are as many civil services as there are departments and offices, and that votes of confidence/no confidence in the civil service may not apply across the board.

It would, however, be unwise for any department to assume that, merely because it does not feature — or features only minimally — in the Ombudsman's lists, it can distance itself from the issue of confidence in the civil service. That issue cannot be assessed solely by reference to the number and nature of complaints to the Ombudsman. There may be aspects of the work of the service which, although unsatisfactory, are of too general a nature to sustain a complaint to the Ombudsman. How alert, for example, is the service in ensuring that the public is aware of its entitlements to social services and tax reliefs? How alert is it in identifying changing trends which point to the need for changes in policy? Tom Barrington has put the issue forcibly: 'There seems to be no grasp of just how remarkably backward we are, and have long been, as compared with other countries in relation to systems for coping with the problems of redress, secrecy and privacy, of how our refusal to face this issue has contributed to the extraordinary degree of public distrust of our administrative system. How long can a democracy survive with such public distrust on the one hand and such administrative apathy on the other?' (Barrington, 1985).

Naught for our comfort there!

HOW OPINIONS ARE FORMED

For most people their opinion of, and therefore their confidence in, the civil service is determined by their experiences at the hands of civil servants. Others may be influenced by the perspective of the civil service presented by outside observers. It is unfortunate that this perspective is rarely based on detailed knowledge of, or adequate research into, the civil service. 'We have', admits Professor J.J. Lee, 'singularly little scholarly analysis of "the state". . . If we believe that superior policy formulation is one way to narrow the economic gap, to say nothing about social and cultural gaps, between the (European Economic) Community and ourselves, then academia must review the manner in which it can most effectively contribute to policy studies' (Lee, 1984).

The only objective, comprehensive, and well researched analysis of the civil service is that provided by the report of the Public Services Organisation Review Group 1966-1969 (the Devlin report). The Group concluded that: 'For all the charges made against it, the civil service has worked with reasonable efficiency. It has served different Governments loyally and with regard to the national interest. In its long established tradition, it operates impartially. It has tried as best it could within the framework of its organization and resources to promote the development of the nation; it has given its advice to Ministers fairly and honestly and, when given the final decisions of the Government, it has implemented them without reservation. The civil service has contributed much to what is progressive in our national life.' (Para 11.2.1).

Of course the Report did not stop there. It proceeded to list quite a number of significant weaknesses — general and fundamental, structural, organisational and management, personnel and planning — and concluded that '. . . the faults are largely those of institutions. Where there has been a failure, it has been in the reluctance to recognise the need for action on the institutions as a whole. . .' (Para. 11.9.1).

There is no academic counterpart, macro or micro, to Devlin. True, there is Fanning's *History of the Department of Finance* but this, as the title makes clear, is confined to one department and concentrates mainly on issues of policy. As an ex-Finance official, I must leave it to others to judge whether the citizenry would have more/less/any confidence in the department after reading Fanning.

The lack of scholarly analysis has not inhibited some academics from making sweeping generalisations about the civil service. Thus, in the course of a single article, Professor Lee resorts to such clichés as 'mandarin disdain', 'bureaucratic centralism', 'a moribund administration' and 'the grip of the bureaucratic state' (Lee, 1985a) — all reminiscent of his reference elsewhere to 'an arthritic public service'.[38] Other academics differ only in their choice of cliché. For Alan Matthews, for example, public administration is a 'creaking machinery' (Matthews, 1983). For Michael Peillon, civil servants are the 'docile instruments of political authorities' (Peillon, 1982). For R.K. McCarthy, they pursue a 'cautious conservative policy' (McCarthy, 1983). Citizens can hardly be blamed for taking these and many similar expressions as the product of informed scholarly insights into the civil service and failing to perceive that, lacking an academic basis, they are as valid or as invalid as the opinions of laymen.

It is of course arguable that the views of academics are quite irrelevant in the context of the citizen's confidence in the civil service. It is equally arguable that Ministerial tributes to the civil service have little effect on the public's perception of the service. The cynics will argue that either Ministers are acting out of a misguided loyalty to the service or that they and the service must hang together or else they will hang separately. The civil service is perhaps entitled to ask the cynics to pay as much or as little attention to Ministerial tributes as to lay criticisms from outsiders. As some commentators have criticised the performance of the civil service in the EEC, let me quote what the Taoiseach, Dr. FitzGerald, has to say in that regard: 'After our Presidency (1975) was over, I made fairly penetrating enquiries as to how our presidency of the different committees and working groups (190 in all) had turned out, and could find no complaints from any source. Many of our chairmen had performed magnificently, the vast majority of them well and none less than adequately' (Smith, 1985).

CONCERN ABOUT REPUTATION

Over-concern about one's reputation can damage that reputation. Disregard of unjustified attacks can undermine confidence or lead to self-fulfilling criticism. Striking a balance between these extremes should not be too difficult for civil servants — particularly if they bear in mind what Clement Attlee said some forty years ago: 'the civil servant soon learns that sufference is the badge of all his tribe' (Attlee, 1954). Attlee's remark is applicable not only to the British civil service (to which he was referring) but to civil services generally. For example: 'From the time of Balzac (Les Employés) denigration of the civil service has been a national sport (in France)... Belgium and Norway... regard their public services with that half-contemptuous, half-patronising indifference the British have for their local officials' (Chapman, 1966).

Germany seems to be the exception. 'The German public official has a status unique in Western Europe. His position comes partly from the German trust of the expert... the German bureaucracy is not simply a body of people providing public services but the living embodiment of the state' (*ibid*).

Heine has argued that some countries are temperamentally monarchical (e.g. Germany) and others republican (e.g. France), and have different attitudes to authority. In its attitude to the civil service, Ireland is firmly in the republican camp.

7

Better Elsewhere?

This articles first appeared in Seirbhís Phoiblí *Vol. 8, No. 2, 1987*

A critic of public administration in Ireland may well wonder whether they order these things better in France — and elsewhere. He may wonder whether, if so, it is because systems elsewhere are better, or whether *individuals* elsewhere are (by and large) better than here. If he is wise, he will accept that it is difficult to distinguish between these two aspects. Better, perhaps, to start with identifying the many differences in the framework within which public administration is operated here and in other comparable countries. Even this limited approach can be superficial (because of an imperfect understanding of the political, social and other influences in the countries in question) and subjective (since the choice of comparisons may be influenced by one's own experience), but it may have its uses in helping to a better understanding of the administrative process, in suggesting some changes that might be opportune, or even in confirming the wisdom of some of our practices. A brief article such as this can, however, provide little more than an outline of even this limited approach.

THREE FACTORS

Any comparison between public administration in Ireland and in Continental Europe must take account of three factors which determine the framework within which public administration is conducted; these are the role of Parliament, the system of administrative law, and the freedom or otherwise of civil servants to engage in politics.

Role of parliament

In a recent essay, Sir Kenneth Clucas (a former Deputy Secretary of the Civil Service Department and Permanent Secretary of the Department of Trade) examined the significance for the British Civil Service of the greater influence of Parliament in that country compared with those elsewhere in Europe (Clucas, 1982). His approach is of particular interest to us in Ireland, given the extent to which our political and administrative systems have been influenced by Britain. Although his comparisons are made with a broad brush, and do not include Ireland, it is reasonable to accept that his conclusions in regard to Britain are, by and large, applicable to this country.

Sir Kenneth claims that the key to understanding the British system of government '. . . lies in the historical fact that (in Britain) political reform preceded administrative reform whereas elsewhere in Europe the opposite was the case.' He argues that '. . . in no other (West European) country does the role of Parliament and the involvement in it of Ministers, match that to be found in (Britain).' Other European parliaments sit for only a fraction of the time of the House of Commons; Ministers in some countries (e.g. France, Netherlands) cannot or need not be Members of Parliament; MPs elsewhere do not exercise the same constituency role as in Britain. He concludes that '. . . the influence which the United Kingdom Parliament has on the conduct of Government, and so on the nature and behaviour of the civil service, is both profound and of a kind not typical elsewhere.'

Sir Kenneth draws many stimulating conclusions from these comparisons; not least the importance of the concept of ministerial responsibility in Britain and the need for the generalist administrator as adviser to Ministers. The cynic may dismiss his analysis as a devious justification for the generalist administrator, but I suggest that it raises issues which it would be unwise to ignore in any comparison among European systems of public administration.

Administrative law

Irish experience is more akin to British, and dissimilar from Continental experience, in another respect. The system of administrative law which obtains in most European countries has had, not surprisingly, a marked influence on public administration. In some of those countries public administration is regarded primarily as the application of law, not the exercise of discretion (Ridley, 1979). In Italy for example, it has led to the concept of the *Stato di Diretto* — the state based on law — in which the exercise of public powers is subjected to a series of tight legal controls which are intended both to form a guarantee against arbitrary executive action and to give authority to the actions of even the lowest level of officialdom (*ibid,* 179). In Germany this approach led to the rejection of the concept of the Ombudsman on the grounds that the civil service acts either legally or illegally — there was no third possibility (*ibid,* 153). The French have not been quite so dogmatic; a modified version of the Ombudsman — the Mediateur — has been introduced (Fry, 1981, 182).

One observer has suggested that in administrative law countries, 'particularly where the higher civil service is legally qualified, notions of responsibility are likely to develop which are at variance with the doctrine of ministerial responsibility. In such cases officials may see their first duty to application of laws, their first commitment a judicial frame of mind in the execution of their duties. They may thus consider a large part of administration as the non-political application of laws and thus as their own preserve in which the politican, though he may intervene, remains an intruder' (Ridley, 1983).

Civil servants and politics

The gap between administration and politics, which is quite marked in Ireland, is much narrower in mainland Europe where civil servants are not expected or required to be political eunuchs. In many cases, European civil servants make no secret of their political affiliations. In some countries indeed they run for Parliament and, if elected, are allowed indefinite leave (France, Netherlands, Italy, Spain) or may remain in office (Denmark, Sweden, Austria, Finland) (Chapman, 1966). This attitude towards politics has an important effect on the European civil service. For example, one may well wonder whether the Continental *cabinet* system — regarded by some in this country as a desirable import — could function effectively without it, since many of those employed in *cabinets* are serving civil servants, chosen primarily because their politics are congenial to their Ministers. Couple this with the fact that few departments in Europe are headed by the Irish equivalent of Secretary-General, so that clashes of jurisdiction and power between the *Chef de Cabinet* and an official head of the department do not arise. Indeed, where, exceptionally, there is a Secretary General, the *cabinet* system works less effectively.

INTERNAL FRAMEWORK

The discussion so far has turned on differences in what might be called the external, institutional, framework, within which the civil service works here and elsewhere. What about differences in the internal framework?

At first sight, it might appear that the Irish framework is much the same as that obtaining in a typical *Western* country — in such respects, for example, as entry by competitive examination, security of tenure, and pensions on retirement. Closer inspection however, reveals some interesting differences.

Pay at the top
Take pay, for example — a subject rarely of indifference to *any* employee. Leaving aside such questions as the differing bases for determining civil service pay in general and how such pay compares across frontiers, it is interesting to look at the arrangements for determining pay at the top. In France, where civil service pay is determined by reference to an index, almost nobody at the top of the scale would receive less than twice the amount indicated by the nominal index; salaries are virtually personalised (Ridley, 1979, 97). In Italy official pay levels bear little relationship to actual earnings which, at the top, are more than double the *official* figure (*ibid*). In Canada, for the top posts '. . . they have a method of reward, within a minimum and a maximum, which is kept confidential to the recipients — there can be a 20% disparity in salary for people in charge of same level departments. The permanent heads of the control

departments advise the Prime Minister who makes the decision each year' (Burns, 1982, 38). This makes our Devlin framework look both fussy and inflexible — but mercifully impersonal.

Non-pay expenditure
A recent editorial in this journal suggested — deliberately provocatively — that control of public non-pay expenditure should be transferred from the Department of Finance to the Department of the Public Service, to be re-named the Department of Public Management.[39] This prompts the question — how do they order these matters elsewhere? In Britain, the Treasury lost control over payroll costs to the Civil Service Department when the latter Department was established in 1969 and regained control when the Civil Service Department was abolished in 1981. In Canada, both pay and non-pay aspects of public expenditure come within the bailie-wick of the Treasury Board.[40] The USA approach seeks a compromise (whether it achieves it is another matter). The Bureau of the Budget controls non-pay expenditure; the Civil Service Commission is responsible for all personnel issues, other than pay; public sector pay is controlled jointly, by the two organisations.[41]

Staffing
Our White Paper, *Serving the Country Better,* proposes that the responsibility of Secretaries for the management of their Departments will be emphasised by empowering them (or other nominated officers) to appoint staff (up to HEO level) and to dismiss staff (up to Clerical Officer level). This falls short of the responsibility given to line departments in some other countries. In Britain, where personnel policy was unified and centralized in 1919, the wheel has almost come full circle and Departments are now responsible for 95% of direct-entry recruitment without any reference to the Civil Service Commission (Fry, 1985, 153). Somewhat similar arrangements operate in Italy and the Netherlands (Ridley, 1979).

Promotion
However much they may differ in regard to other aspects of personnel policy, many countries face a common problem in

regard to one aspect, promotion policy. As one author has put it, 'There is, in fact, a genuine dilemma in promotion which has caused all countries concern over the last twenty or thirty years. How to ensure reasonable prospects of advancement to all officials, and at the same time protect the public's interest in having posts filled by the most able men. . . . Some countries still continue to put the major emphasis throughout the service on seniority. . . . there is fear amongst public service personnel — reinforced by long memories — that any substantial breach in the seniority rule will open the door to widespread promotion on political and personal grounds' (Chapman, 1966, 164, 166). The hard-pressed citizen might well ruefully recall Kipling's phrase that the Colonel's lady and Judy O'Grady are sisters, under their skins. He might, however, take some comfort from the fact that the reference is over twenty years old; a more recent survey might show a different picture.

AUSTRALIAN EXPERIENCE

The administration-watcher will find some recent developments in Australia of particular interest. The following summary of these developments is taken from an analysis by Dr John Griffiths, Director of Research of the Australian Administrative Review Council:[42]

● The enactment in 1975 of the Administrative Appeals Tribunal Act which establishes (a) the Administrative Appeals Tribunal (AAT) as a general appeals tribunal to review certain administrative decisions on their merits and obliges decision makers to provide upon request a written statement of reasons for a reviewable decision; and (b) the Administrative Review Council (ARC) as a permanent and independent advisory body responsible for monitoring a wide range of matters relating to review of administrative decisions and giving advice to the government on those matters. The AAT commenced operations on 1 July 1976 and the Council held its first meeting in December 1976.

● The enactment in 1976 of the Ombudsman Act which sets up the office of the Commonwealth ombudsman to investigate complaints of defective administration by federal departments and authorities. The first and current ombudsman is Professor Jack Richardson (formerly Robert Garran Professor of Constitutional Law at the Australian National University), who took office on 1 July 1977.

● The enactment in 1977 of the Administrative Decisions (Judicial Review) Act which establishes a relatively simple form of procedure in the Federal Court of Australia for obtaining judicial review of administrative decisions. The Act codifies the grounds of review and also obliges administrators to provide upon request a statement of reasons for a reviewable decision. The Act was passed in 1977 but it did not commence operation until 1 October 1980.

● The enactment in 1982 of the Freedom of Information Act which creates a legal right of access to documents in the possession of federal departments and authorities. Certain categories of documents are exempt from disclosure. The Act also requires federal agencies to publish information about their operations and powers and to make publicly available any manuals or internal guidelines used in decision making. The Act came into operation on 1 December 1982.

In Dr. Griffith's words, 'these measures represent a package of reforms which is designed to regulate the relationship between government and individuals and to reconcile the potential conflict of interest between providing efficient and effective public administration and safeguarding rights of individual justice.'

Of all these measures the one which would strike the outsider as the most far-reaching is the Administrative Appeals Tribunal and indeed, it is described by Dr. Griffiths as 'one of the most radical and innovative aspects of recent reforms in Australia.' Two features in particular are notable: the obligation on decision makers to provide upon request a written statement of reasons for a reviewable decision, and the power of the Tribunal to determine what is the correct or preferable decision even though such a decision is in conflict with departmental non-statutory policy — a power which, incidentally, derives not from the governing legislation but rather from a series of Court decisions. Commenting on this aspect of the Tribunal, one commentator warned that 'Unless an arrangement can be found which acknowledges and upholds the superiority of decisions openly arrived at consistent with the law, by elected officials, it would seem likely that the Administrative Appeal Tribunal will atrophy or be confined to a very limited class of case' (Kirby, 1981). In fact the Tribunal has exercised this power with considerable self-restraint and, according to Dr. Griffiths, has avoided 'significant problems concerning compliance with policy considerations', while still finding in favour of almost one-half of the applications before them.

An aspect of particular interest to public servants *qua* employees is that amongst the areas of greatest usage of the power to seek a review of decisions has been promotion and disciplinary decisions within the public service. Well over one-half of the promotion appeals have been successful!

These Australian changes have involved considerable cost, both in financial and staff resource terms, but Dr. Griffiths claims that, because administrators have had to review and improve their decision-making procedures, the quality of decisions has improved.

Whether or not the right balance has been struck between efficiency and equity/justice can only be established by a detailed study — the results of which would be of considerable interest to Irish citizens and administrators alike.

It is not possible in a short article to do more than select a few examples to show that, in other countries, the external and internal influences on public administration differ from those in this country — hardly a surprising conclusion. Nor is it possible to draw any inference from these examples regarding the quality and efficiency of public administration in the countries in question. Perhaps indeed we can say no more than — in the pragmatic words of Deng Xiaoping — 'It doesn't matter if the cat is black or white as long as it catches mice'.

8

The Top Level Appointments Committee

This article first appeared in Seirbhís Phoiblí, *Vol. 9, No. 1, 1988*

If the calibre of the senior grades in the civil service is a major influence on the efficiency and effectiveness of the service, then it is arguable that the establishment of the Top Level Appointments Committee (TLAC) was one of the most important decisions taken in the area of public administration. This note traces the background to this decision, summarises the senior appointments made since the Committee was established, and draws some conclusions regarding the results achieved.

In any large, hierarchical organisation such as the civil service, the basis on which promotions should be made is often a matter of disagreement, if not of conflict. Typically the disagreement and conflict reflect the differing weights to be accorded, in practice, to seniority on the one hand, and to merit on the other. This is an issue which is rarely discussed objectively, not least because there is so little published data. The Report of the Public Services Organisation Review Group (the Devlin Report) analysed total promotions in general service grades in all departments in the years 1960, 1963 and 1966, with the results shown in Table 3:

Table 3: **Total promotions analysed**

Year	Total promotions	Senior officers promoted
1960	154	37
1963	107	22
1966	146	41

The Devlin Group concluded that:

> These tables indicate that seniority is not the absolute criterion for promotion in the civil service that is sometimes alleged but, if allowance is made for the fact that unpromotable officers will rise to the top of the seniority lists, the weight given to seniority, *in some Departments* becomes apparent.

It might be added however, that the figures provide no basis for the gibe of 'indentured' promotion levelled against the civil service as a whole.

Since the Devlin Report, attempts have been made to throw open senior posts to service-wide competition. Over an extended period these attempts met with only limited success. Furthermore, inter-departmental competition did not extend to posts above the level of Principal Officer. Finally, while many appointments to Assistant Secretary, Deputy Secretary and Secretary posts paid no homage to seniority, there were undoubtedly exceptions where seniority seemed to be the dominating criterion. What Cardinal Agostino Casaroli, Vatican Secretary of State, said of himself — with tongue in cheek, no doubt — rings a familiar bell: 'Promotion to the rank of under-secretary came by the natural process of being there and growing older'.[43]

In its Programme of December 1982, the Coalition Government headed by Dr Garret FitzGerald undertook that there would be open competition for *certain* (unspecified) 'top civil service jobs'. The decision, twelve months later, to establish the TLAC marked a significant modification of this commitment. While the new system does accommodate open competition, its main element is automatic inter-departmental competition for Assistant Secretary posts and higher (including non-general service grades). The Committee's remit does not extend to vacancies arising in the Department of Foreign Affairs (at all relevant levels) or, it appears, to vacancies in the Office of the Revenue Commissioners (Chairman and Commissioners). Only the Chairman is exempted because he must be a Commissioner but a recent promotion to Commissioner did not go via TLAC. There is no public explanation for these exclusions.

The main features of the new system are:

● The Committee consists of the Secretary to the Government, the Secretary (Public Service Management and Development). Department of Finance, two Secretaries of Departments chosen by the Taoiseach after consultation with the Minister for Finance (the Departments at present represented are Environment and Transport and Tourism), the Chairman for the time being of the Public Service Advisory Council — the present incumbent being Dr Liam St J Devlin — and, on an ad hoc basis, the outgoing Secretary of a Department, for the appointment of his successor.

● The Committee's recommendations are addressed to the Government (in the case of Secretaries) and to the Minister of the Department concerned (in the case of other grades). Only one recommendation is made in respect of each vacancy but, in an important change made following the change of Government in 1987, three recommendations are now made in the case of vacancies at Secretary (or equivalent) level; the names are *not* ranked in order of preference.

● In picking the best person for the post, the Committee is required to do so irrespective of Departmental background or speciality. The objective is to promote inter-departmental mobility and to end the dual structure of professional and non-professional career streams.

● The Committee is free to recommend that any particular post be filled by open competition. The Committee made two such recommendations. Open Competitions were held under TLAC auspices for a post of Assistant Secretary in the Department of Finance and an Assistant Secretary post in the Department of the Public Service. The posts were filled under TLAC auspices using the Civil Service Commission i.e. a number of TLAC members were on the selection board.

● No public information is available as to whether the Committee's recommendations were in all cases accepted by the Government and Ministers concerned. Rumour has it that one recommendation involving an Assistant Secretary post in the Department of Defence was not accepted.

So much for the broad structure of the new approach. Before discussing the results, it is useful to look at the procedures adopted by the Committee, since these can have a bearing on the results:

● In the case of all officers coming within the ambit of the Committee, there is available a curriculum vitae prepared by the officer and an assessment report completed by the officer's Department. Appraisals make provision for Ministerial views; it is not known to what extent these have been sought/provided, or whether there are any significant differences between Departments in this respect.

● Applications are invited for each vacancy as it arises.

● The head of the Department in which the vacancy has arisen is involved (with the Committee) in the process of discussing the merits of each applicant — but presumably has no vote except for the appointment of his successor.

● The Committee prepares a short-list from the applications received. The applicants on the short-list are referred to the Civil Service Commission for interview. The Committee, in making its recommendations, has on occasion gone outside the list submitted to it by the Civil Service Commission.

● The Secretary of the Department in which the vacancy occurs is invited to nominate *one* applicant from that Department who will meet the Committee without going through the Civil Commission process; this number was later increased to *two*. The facility is availed of in almost all cases. To what extent have successful candidates been selected from among officers nominated in this way?

The Committee has been surprisingly active since it commenced operations in January 1984. In the period to mid

1987, 67 appointments coming within its ambit have been made. These break down as follows:

Secretary (including one Second Secretary, Department of Finance)	13
Assistant Secretary (including two Deputy Secretaries)	43
Other (professional, specialist posts)	11
	67

The vacancies in question arose in all Departments and major offices, with the exception of the Department of the Taoiseach, the Department of Energy and the Office of Public Works. On an *ad hoc* basis, a vacancy for the post of Secretary, Department of Finance in 1987 was filled without recourse to the Committee.

Three issues, in particular, arise in relation to the work of the Committee; the extent to which it has fostered inter-departmental mobility; its success or otherwise in helping to abolish the 'dual structure'; finally, and most importantly, how successful the scheme has been, what difference it has made.

MOBILITY

In assessing the Committee's record under this heading, it is necessary to exclude three entries because they relate to small offices (Stationery Office, Civil Service Commission and the Farm Tax Commission) where the concept of mobility is of limited relevance. This leaves 64 entries. Of these, seventeen involved promotions across Departmental boundaries and 47 involved promotions within the Departments in which the vacancies occured. A breakdown of these figures yields some interesting results (see Table 4).

Table 4: **Promotions mobility**

	Vacancy Filled Outside Dept.	Inside Dept.	Total
'Generalist' Posts (Assistant Secretary, Deputy Secretary, Secretary)	16	38	54
Professional, Technical or Specialist Posts	1	9	10
Total	17	47	64

The one professional, technical or specialist vacancy filled from outside the Department was the exception that proved the rule; the officer in question had earlier made a move in the opposite direction.

Of the 'generalist' service posts, sixteen, or about 30% of the total, involved trans-Departmental promotions. When this group is further broken down between (a) Secretaries and equivalent and (b) Deputy and Assistant Secretaries, the percentage rises to almost 40% (5 out of 13) for (a) and falls to 27% (11 out of 41) for (b).

A further analysis of the figures (see Table 5) yields more interesting results:

Table 5: **Departments with greatest numbers of promotees**

Dept.	Promotions within the department	Promotions outside department	Total	Departmental posts filled by outsiders
Finance	4	7	11	—
Justice	7	1	8	—
Public Service	3	5	8	1
Revenue	7	—	7	2
Environment	5	—	5	—
Agriculture	3	1	4	1
	29	14	43	4
All other Depts. (11) and Offices (3)	19	5	24	15
Total*	48	19	67	19

*Includes posts in the Stationery Office, Civil Service Commission and Farm Tax Commission excluded from preceding table.

Six institutions (five Departments, one Office) accounted for about two thirds of the total promotions and for over 70% of the promotions crossing departmental boundaries. Included in these figures are nine of the eleven professional etc. posts filled in the period covered by the Table; all but one of these eleven posts were filled from within. It is these inclusions which must be taken into consideration in considering the Justice and Revenue figures above; these include three and five posts respectively of a professional, etc., nature.

The other significant point to emerge from the Table is that twelve of the nineteen promotions which crossed departmental boundaries involved officers from Finance (7) and Public Service (5). Only *one* other Department (Communications with two) accounted for more than one trans – Departmental promotion.

THE DUAL STRUCTURE

The issue here is the extent to which the new system facilitated the promotion of general service officers (or Departmental grades) to professional, technical or specialist grades — and vice versa. On this test, the new system has not, so far, borne out the claim made at its announcement that it would 'bring to an end the dual structure — a system by which professional and non-professionals have their own structures.' Of the eleven vacancies in professional etc. posts which were filled since January 1984, none was filled by a non-professional, technical or specialist officer. Of the 56 'generalist' posts, four (in Defence, Education, Revenue and Public Service) were filled by officers with professional, technical or specialist backgrounds. Perhaps the log jam is being broken, but in one direction only, and slowly.

APPRAISAL

Although the Committee has been quite active since it was established (perhaps reflecting, in part, the growing tendency of senior civil servants to retire before 65 years) it is too soon to reach firm conclusions about its work, since the critical test — its success in selecting the best people for promotion — can be assessed (if at all) only over a longer time-span. Some provisional comments however may be in order.

The TLAC system seems by now to have become an accepted part of life at the top of the civil service, despite initial problems caused by the failure to consult departments and staff before its introduction. It is not known what changes were made in the operation of the system to accommodate views from staff and departments; perhaps the exceptions made for the Department of Foreign Affairs and, it seems, the Office of the Revenue Commissioners, the right to nominate one, and later two, Departmental officers to appear before the Committee without going through the CSC procedure, and the submission of three names in the case of vacancies for secretaries, are examples of such modifications.

The Committee has achieved some success in promoting inter-departmental mobility at senior level, but the record is hardly outstanding, except perhaps at Secretary level. Given the trend towards inter-departmental competition at Assistant Principal and Principal Officer level, before the Committee was established, it would be wrong to conclude that the process would not have been extended at some stage to Assistant Secretary level, with results perhaps not too far short of that achieved by TLAC. Extension to Secretary level, were it to happen, would have been a major break-through and would undoubtedly have taken much longer — but this would have been no harm for, as I have argued elsewhere (see 'Serving the Country Better' in this book), it might perhaps have been better if the TLAC scheme had *not* included Secretary posts within its ambit, right from the outset. I note that Thomas Balogh, a stern critic of the British civil service, had reservations about inter-departmental mobility at the top — reservations which reflected his criticism of the 'gifted amateur' image of the British civil service:

Advice to the Prime Minister and to the Cabinet on highest appointments in the civil service should be tendered by a committee of civil servants. In the main, shifts between departments should be exceptional and subject to detailed explanation to the Cabinet (Balogh, 1968).

What significance should be attached to the fact that only two open competitions have been held for posts coming within the ambit of the Committee? Is this a comment on the merit of the civil service applicants, or a recognition of the fact that the salaries offered would not be attractive? It is significant that, of five senior posts in the Department of the Public Service for which open competitions were held in the period from 1972 to 1979, only one was filled from outside the service (Whelan, 1983); the two open competitions held under TLAC auspices were filled from within the Departments concerned.

The TLAC system has not removed the main difficulty in selecting the best people for promotion, it has merely given more people an opportunity of applying for the vacant posts. The main difficulty is, of course, that of assessment, both an art and a science in which civil servants (and many, many others) do not excel. This is not simply a matter of filling in forms; indeed form-filling can lead to the danger of mistaking the shadow for the substance. I do not know whether any special measures were taken to enhance the assessment process or, equally important, to ensure inter-departmental coherence in that process. The Committee is, not surprisingly, aware of the problem of inter-departmental variations. They point out, somewhat coyly, that they 'are in a position to identify different ranking patterns in different departments'. The problem is compounded by the fact that peer-assessment is often the most reliable assessment; the difficulty is how best to use this in inter-departmental competitions. It would be interesting to know whether, and, if so, how often, the Committee's recommendations have run counter to peer-group assessments.

It may be argued that assessment problems are resolved during the interviews held by the CSC and by the Committee. This issue must remain unresolved in the absence of information about the interviewing procedures adopted for TLAC purposes. It remains true of course, that high-fliers will come to the top, almost regardless of the standard or type of interview, but this does not alter the fact that, for these posts, only the best type of interview is satisfactory.

Initially there was some hostility to the new system of promotion because it was feared that youth would be preferred to experience, giving a civil service slant to the bitter truth of being too old at forty or so. Under the new system some quite young officers have gained promotion — but so did a number who had long lost the first flush of youth. It must be remembered that before 1984 there were quite a number of 'out-of-turn' promotions, including some about the same age as those who gained their spurs since 1984. It would not be surprising however if the average age of promotees has fallen since 1984. Would it be too much an intrusion on privacy if the age of promotees were indicated?[44]

An integral part of the new system was the stipulation that Secretaries appointed under it would serve for a period of not more than seven years; there were special arrangements for officers aged 55 years and over when the scheme started. This stipulation no doubt reflected the pressures at the top and the danger of burnt-out cases. Although the scheme is nearly four years old, a decision has not yet been made, or, if made, not published, about the conditions of service of Secretaries whose seven-year term has ended.

CONCLUSION

The number and level of promotions involved in the TLAC system makes that system one of the most important factors in the civil service. Although some of the claims made for the system on its introduction have yet to be validated, it is undeniable that life at the top has been changed radically. If it is competition that makes Sammy run, then the civil service pace has undoubtedly quickened. It would be wrong to overlook the disappointment, frustration and pain of those who have been 'also ran'; it would be unwise to neglect the danger that this may lead to some apathy and lack of commitment, and it would be unfair not to hold out some hope to that much under-rated official, the person whose talents were rated 'average'. But, overall, the change has surely been for the better.

In a recent survey of the public service in Western and North European countries, Professor Leemans concluded that 'There is a clear and almost universal shift towards emphasis on quality rather than on seniority. Routine promotions are diminishing. Recent public personnel policy statements in several countries have stressed the importance of competition within the Civil Service (Leemans, 1987, 63-88). It is gratifying to know that, in this respect at least, we are abreast of best practice elsewhere.

9

Public Employment Observed*

This paper first appeared in Seirbhís Phoiblí *Vol. 10, No. 2, 1989*

The size of the public sector is often a cause for concern, given its cost to the Exchequer. Questions are asked as to whether the Irish public sector is appropriate to the size of the overall working population. In considering such questions it may help to place public employment in Ireland in an international setting.

COMPARISONS AND DEFINITIONS

Public employment comparisons between countries and over time are, however, hampered by definitional problems. The, heading 'public administration and defence' in the EC Labour Force Surveys excludes employment in such areas as health, education, postal services and transport. The OECD heading 'general government' excludes government-owned firms and state corporations which produce and sell goods on the market. Two recent studies by Professor Richard Rose (Rose, 1980, 1986) avoid these difficulties by adopting a comprehensive definition of public employment. The definition is not precisely the same in the two studies, but there is not any substantial difference in the approach adopted. Public employment, according to the earlier (1980) study, includes

---

*This article was sent for publication before Dr William K. O'Riordan's paper, 'Is Irish Public Employment a Burden?' was read before the Statistical and Social Enquiry Society of Ireland (26 Oct. 1989).

persons working full-time or part-time for a government agency, that is an institution headed by elected officials or by appointees of an elected government; or principally owned by government and/or principally funded by government grants.

It is understandable that the labours of data-collection have restricted the scope of Professor Rose's studies — the earlier one (1980) to five countries, the later one (1986) to six countries, including four from the first study. It is fortunate for those who would wish to place Irish public employment in an (admittedly restricted) international setting that Ireland is included in the 1980 study.

While Ireland is not included in Rose's later study, it is possible to update his public employment/labour force figure for Ireland by reference to Peter Humphries' study (Humphries, 1983). Humphries' definition of public employment seems to be almost as comprehensive as Rose's, as can be seen by comparing their figures for 1978 (Rose, 296,000 and Humphries, 287,500), although rather disconcertingly there is a marked difference between their labour force figures for Ireland for that year with Rose giving 1,148,000 and Humphries 1,195,000.

Humphries' figures for public employment and labour force in 1983 are 324,700 and 1,299,000 respectively, which give a public employment/labour force percentage of 25.0%; his public employment figure for 1983 is fairly close to that — 321,752 — of Michael Ross for that year (Ross, 1983).

Inserting this percentage in a table which amalgamates figures from Rose's two studies gives the result shown in Table 6:

Table 6: **Public sector employment as percentage of labour force**

	1951	*1976*	*1981*
Sweden	21.0	32.4	38.2
Britain	26.4	30.5	31.4
Ireland	14.5	25.8	25.0
Italy	10.3	22.3	24.4
USA	16.4	18.5	18.3
France	17.5	N/A	32.6
Germany	14.4	N/A	25.8

The precise years to which the figures relate differ from country to country but fall within the ranges 1950-1953, 1975-1978 and 1980-1983. The Irish figures relate to 1953, 1978 and 1983.

The '1951' data for Sweden, Britain, Italy and USA are taken from the 1980 study. The 1986 study gives slightly different figures for 1951 for the last three countries named but an incredibly large difference (15.2% as against 21.0%) for Sweden. The explanation can hardly lie in the fact that the base year for the 1980 study was 1952 and that for the 1986 study was 1950.

Not surprisingly, the USA is the only exception to the substantial increase in the public employment/labour force ratio over the three decades covered by the Table. Of the seven countries for which '1951' and '1981' figures are available the rate of increase was third lowest in Ireland. Of the five countries for which '1976' and '1981' figures are available, the upward trend in the ratio was reversed in only two — Ireland and the USA.

Of the countries surveyed, Ireland is undoubtedly the poorest and the smallest. In the absence of a study of the relationship between per capita GNP, size, and the level of public administration, it is not possible to say how these factors have affected the Irish figures — if at all. It is interesting to note that the public employment ratio is exceptionally low for a rich country like the USA — but also exceptionally high for a rich country such as Sweden.

Two bases are sometimes used in calculating the public employment ratio — the labour force (as in this article) and the non-agricultural labour force. I see little point in adopting the second base, unless a correction were made in the public employment figures in respect of the public officials (teachers, health and social welfare personnel etc.) employed in servicing the non-agricultural sector.

It might be argued that comparisons should take account of the low Irish defence expenditure and the high Irish dependency figures. In the absence, however, of information regarding any distorting aspects in the data for other countries, it is preferable not to adjust any of the figures.

Professor Rose's studies do more than bring together comprehensive and comparable public employment data for a number of countries. He subjects the figures to a wide-ranging and searching analysis and it is this, rather than the raw disaggregated data, which makes his studies compelling reading. I do not propose to traverse the ground so ably covered by him. My interest is in the ways in which Ireland differs from, or is similar to, the other countries surveyed. I reproduce here the main tables in the 1980 study, confining these to the data for the 'latest year', referred to for convenience as '1976', although the figures for the USA and Sweden relate to 1975 and for Ireland to 1978 (Tables 7=13).

Table 7: Percentage of public employment by category — 1976

	Social programmes	Mobilising economic resources	Defining responsibilities of government
	(a)	(b)	(c)
Sweden	55.9	23.7	20.4
Britain	40.6*	37.7	14.7
Ireland	39.6	47.2	13.2
Italy	40.5	39.3	20.2
USA	54.4	15.6	30.0

(a) Education, health, social services.
(b) Transportation, post, telephone, telegraph, nationalised industries, roads etc.
(c) External defence, internal order, managing finances, judical activities.
*This should read 47.6
This table is an amalgamation of Tables 3, 4 and 5 in the Rose study. A residual item, other programmes and administration, has been excluded in calculating the percentages.

It is clear from Rose's analysis, and from Humphries' detailed examination of the Irish position, that public employment is extremely heterogeneous. Generalisations regarding public employment must be treated with reserve. With this warning in mind, what can we say about public employment in Ireland, in the light of Rose's analysis for 1976, which, it must be stressed, covers only five countries?

● Ireland occupied a mid-point position in the ranking of five countries by reference to public employment/labour force ratios. In the 1981 ranking it was third lowest out of seven countries.

● Of the various categories of public employment, Ireland ranked highest in 'Mobilising Economic Resources' and lowest in 'Social Programmes' and 'Defining Responsibilities of Government'.

When public employment is analysed by type or organisation, Ireland ranked highest in respect of 'Central Government' and second lowest in respect of 'Local Government'.

Table 8: **Distribution of public employment by type of organization — 1976**

	Central Government %	Local Government %	Neither %
Sweden	35	30	35
Britain	30	38	32
Ireland	42	25	33
Italy	39	15	46
USA	24	50	26

The percentage of 'qualified' manpower in public employment in Ireland was second lowest (out of four countries) but the public/private difference in this respect in Ireland was second highest. In fact 54% of qualified manpower in Ireland was in public employment (See Table 9).

Table 9: **Qualified manpower in public and private employment—1976**

	Public %	Private %	Public/ Private Difference %
Britain (1971)	21	11	10
Ireland (1971)	22	5	17
Italy (1971)	33	8	25
USA (1970)	31	16	15

Figures are best regarded as estimates showing orders of magnitude.

Qualifications are defined generally as 'examined and certificated expertise, signifying an above average level of intelligence and normally a particular function competence'. In Ireland's case they are defined as full-time education ceasing at age 19 or later.

Public employment in Ireland was highly trade-unionised, sharing joint highest ranking with Sweden. As regards private employment unionisation, Ireland's ranking was second highest.

Table 10: **Levels of unionisation in public and private employment—1976**

	Public employment %	Private employment %	Difference %
Sweden	81	71	+ 10
Britain	72	34	+ 38
Ireland	81	51	+ 30
Italy	39	39	—
USA	25	27	− 2

When public employment is analysed by reference to the type of output produced (see Table 11), Ireland's ranking in regard to
— Give Away Goods, was second lowest.
— Collective Goods, was second lowest.
— Marketed Goods, was second highest.

Table 11: **Distribution of employment according to type of output produced — 1976**

	Give away goods (a)	Collective goods (b)	Marketed goods (c)
Sweden	55	24	21
Britain	48	16	36
Ireland	45	18	37
Italy	40	22	38
USA	51	41	8

(a) Products provided free of charge or at nominal cost to all eligible to receive them — e.g. social welfare, health, education.
(b) Provided for the benefit of the whole of society — e.g. defence.
(c) Products which provide, at a charge, identifiable goods for identifiable consumers — railways, post office, electricity etc.

In Table 12 women not in the labour force, and students, are not excluded, and the figures therefore are minimum estimates. Private sector employment sustained by government purchases is not included. When ranked by reference to the total numbers receiving primary incomes from Government (whether as public employees or non-working income recipients) Ireland's ranking was third highest — the middle position.

Table 12: **Extent of government provision of primary incomes — 1976**

	Public employees	Non-working income recipients	Total receiving income from government
		as % of total adult population	
Sweden	22	28	49
Britain	20	28	48
Ireland	15	28	43
Italy	12	30	42
USA	12	23	35

Figures show only relative magnitudes.

In an analysis of the sources of positive growth in the labour force (Table 13) Ireland had the highest ranking in respect of the contribution from public employment. (Professor Brendan Walsh has warned that... 'it is mistaken to equate the gross increase in public sector employment with its net contribution to the growth of employment... it is unwise to ignore the possibility that some of the additional public employment merely replaced employment that would have appeared in the private sector')[45]

Table 13: **Sources of positive growth in the labour force 1951-76**

	Public employment %	Private employment Non-agricultural %	Agricultural %	Unemployment %
Sweden	58	42	—	—
Britain	60	—	—	40
Ireland	79	—	—	21
Italy	40	60	—	—
USA	21	62	—	17

Percentages refer to the proportion of all additional persons in those sectors of the labour force where growth has occurred e.g. for Ireland:

Public Employment	+ 114,000 (79%)	
Unemployment	+ 30,000 (21%)	144,000
Private Employment:		
Agricultural	− 231,000	
Non Agricultural	− 17,000	− 248,000
Net fall in labour force		− 104,000

CONCLUSIONS

The broad conclusions regarding public service employment in Ireland which emerge from this (admittedly limited) international review may be summarised as follows:

—The public employment/labour force ratio is somewhat below average.

— While the ratio has increased substantially in recent decades, the rate of increase is, again, somewhat below average and was, in fact, reversed in recent years.

— In recent decades, the contribution of public employment to growth in the labour force was greatest in Ireland.

— Ireland has a high ranking in regard to the percentage of public employment in economic activity and in central government; it has a correspondingly low ranking in regard to the percentage involved in the provision of collective goods.

— Public employment in Ireland is highly trade unionised and attracts over one half of the educationally qualified manpower.

It must be stressed that this analysis in quantitative, not qualitative terms; it tells us nothing, for example, about the efficiency of public employment in Ireland. Professor Rose's study helps us, however, to a better understanding of public employment in Ireland and to an appreciation of how it compares with public employment elsewhere. It is a pity that the analysis is somewhat out of date. It would be worthwhile updating the raw material and subjecting it to a Rose-type analysis; indeed, other aspects, in addition to those studied by Rose, may suggest themselves. Public employment is so important to our community and our economy that more, and more up-to-date, analysis is essential. Analysis should help towards a better understanding of the public service and lead to a more informed debate on its weakness and strengths. It could thus deal a blow to the current Bulverisation of the public service. Ezekiel Bulver, a creation of C.S. Lewis, propounded the 'great truth that refutation is no necessary part of argument. Assume that your opponent is wrong and then explain his error, and the world will be at your feet'.[46] Let us expose the public service Bulvers to another 'great truth' — that of the facts.

10

Ministers, Civil Servants, and Others

The relationship between Ministers and senior civil servants has been described in various ways. To some it is akin to a marriage, to others a partnership. For some, the relationship represents 'the elbow of government' (Chubb 1974) — but thankfully not the armpit! The Minister is said to be the masculine principle, the department the feminine principle, in policy making (Mattei 1973), whatever that may mean. Leaving imagery and metaphor aside, it is evident that any assessment of public administration, of its strengths and weaknesses, must take this relationship into account; an obvious point, but one which is rarely made in this country. A theoretical point, too, since we lack the data on which to test it. Indeed it is doubtful if it would ever be possible, even with extensive research, to distinguish between the contributions made by Ministers and those made by senior civil servants to the administrative process. This article has the more limited objective of identifying some of the factors which have a bearing on this issue — with the emphasis on the role of Ministers, since I have written elsewhere on that of the civil service.

A FRAGMENTED CIVIL SERVICE

If there were one aspect above all else regarding the civil service which I would single out in the present context, it is its fragmented nature. There is a good deal of truth in the saying that there are as many civil services as there are Departments (and Offices) of State. A civil servant does not join 'the civil service', he joins 'a Department'. There are, of course many things that bind Departments together — unified recruitment standards and procedures, common pay structures etc. — but the binding is more superficial than fundamental; it remains to be seen whether TLAC will be a binding agent. To some extent this reflects the competing interests of Ministers in the struggle for funds and for the supremacy of their policies. Too often, however, civil servants have felt it incumbent on them to prolong the battle — at their level — for departmental viewpoints, to fight on long after it was clear that neither side would yield and that the issue could be resolved — if at all — only by the Government. In that sense there is, regrettably, some truth in the accusation that civil servants sometimes make work for each other. I say this with some hesitation, because I run the danger of appearing to give support to Professor Lee's breath-taking contention that 'Rivalries are so intense within many government departments and semi-state institutions, much less between them, that to speak of co-ordinated government at present makes a mockery of language' (Lee, 1973).

Because of its fragmentation, the input of the civil service to the reform (or restructuring, for those who consider that 'reform' is pejorative) of the system has been inadequate. Ironically, the establishment of the Department of the Public Service has given the faint-hearted, the indifferent, or the hostile an excuse for opting out, for 'leaving it to them.' This would have been less easy had there been a greater sense of cohesion in the service. If there had been institutional arrangements e.g. regular meetings of the Secretaries of Departments, it might have been easier to strive for a service-wide commitment to change, or at least for a service-wide consensus on whether change was necessary. In my period as Secretary of the Department of Finance, I can recall only two meetings of Secretaries of Departments (apart of course from pleasant social gatherings when we bid farewell to retiring colleagues) but memory may play me false on this. I remember one Secretary who said he was too busy to attend, and also getting the impression, even if slightly, that such gatherings were a source of wonder, if not of suspicion, to Ministers. I wonder how they would react to the practice in Britain of having weekly meetings of Permanent Secretaries? (Barnett, 1982, 188).

I think that Departmental Secretaries should meet several times a year to discuss issues of service-wide concern*; I would not absolve myself from criticism for not having tried to promote this idea more zealously during my period as Departmental Secretary. In particular I think that Secretaries, as a group, should take an active and positive role in the process of changing the civil service; in effect this means, at this stage, in the implementation of the White Paper *Serving the Country Better* or any variation thereof which experience and further reflection might suggest to be desirable. This involvement in civil service reform should not of course be confined to civil servants who are departmental heads, but it would be regrettable if they were to stand aside from the process. As servants of the State, and as citizens, their duty is clear. I reject as unproven (to put it mildly) Professor Lee's contention that 'if one country falls so far behind so many others over half a century, its administrative arrangements must come under grave suspicion' (Lee, 1985) (the implication being that other 'arrangements' are not suspect). I accept without reservation that civil servants should be active, rather than passive, in the reform of the service in which they work. While I reject as equally unproven (again to put it mildly) Niskanen's stereotype of the self-interested bureaucrats who:

> are primarily motivated by self-interest — budget maximisation is regarded as a reasonable proximation to the maximisation of the bureaucrat's utility (Jackson 1986, 102).

An active, reforming, stance by senior — and all other — civil servants would help to demolish his creaky model.

---

*According to the *Irish Times,* 11 March 1987, there were two meetings of Departmental Secretaries 'to discuss overall policy' in the preceding 18 months.

TOO LARGE A CIVIL SERVICE?

The new Irish State is said to have inherited in 1922 an administrative system based on imperial standards and to have failed to adapt it to the needs of a small economy. I fail to understand the precise basis of this criticism — which, incidentally, hardly does justice to the advantages which the new State derived from the acquisition of a ready-made public administration. According to Nicholas Mansergh:

> Amid the rhetoric that precedes the national revolution and the violence that attends it, it is easy to overlook the dependence of a modern state upon experienced administrators and the equipment without which they cannot function.[47]

It is, of course, arguable that the size of the service taken over in 1922 was too large for the country or, given its size, that we failed to adapt it to meet our needs. I can accept the second point; while recognising that it involves an element of jobbing backwards. As regards the first, I am not aware of any evidence to suggest that the size of the civil service in 1922 was excessive. Such evidence as is available for later years suggests that our public service/labour force ratio was about average compared with other countries (*see* Chapter 9, 'Public Employment Observed'). Certainly the vast increase in the size of the service since 1922 was of our own making and had little to do with the size or structure of the system taken over on the foundation of the State. It is instructive, for example, to compare the number of Departments listed in the Ministers and Secretaries Act 1924 — eleven — with those in existence at present — seventeen. The comparison does not take account of the bewildering changes in the titles and functions of some Departments and the disappearance of others (e.g. Economic Planning and Development) — developments which owed more to political expediency than to administrative rationale. For many people, the answer to a problem is to create a Department to deal with it: if they had their way, we would have Departments to deal solely with tourism, youth, women's affairs, forestry, taxation economic planning. . . .

I am convinced that the civil service would be more efficient and cost-effective if the number of Departments were reduced. In this small country, what justification is there, for example, for having three central Departments of State — Taoiseach's, Public Service and Finance? [In the Government of March 1987, the DPS was merged with the Department of Finance, but the number of departments was not reduced.] More than administrative benefits are involved. There is also the question of the pool of political talent available to head up Departments. Between Ministers and Ministers of State, the present system involves fielding a team of thirty from a total pool which will rarely much exceed eighty. In fact the numbers effectively available are usually much less than eighty, if one excludes new faces, those who (exceptionally) do not wish to offer themselves, and those who just could not be considered. This is not a criticism of politicians; the same comment would apply in the case of any other significant field of endeavour and the same number of participants. The remedy is not to increase the number of TDs; indeed it is difficult to justify the increase of some 30% in the number of TDs since 1922. Restricting the number of Departments would help to achieve a better balance between supply and demand; even if Departments with exceptionally heavy work-loads had to be given two Ministers of State, the net benefit would still be worthwhile. The politician would, no doubt, retort that a price would have to be paid — certain sensitive constituencies would be left without benefit of Ministerial representation.

THE WORK-LOAD ON MINISTERS

It is common ground that the work-load on Ministers is excessive. The sum total of demands on them as party member, constituency representative, member of Government, departmental head, member of EEC Council, etc. is clearly excessive. Ministers could, however, help themselves by not being quite so available to the public. As an ex-civil servant I am not naive enough to suggest that — particularly given our system of multi-member constituencies — they should neglect their constituents. But think of all those functions they attend, of all those deputations they receive, of all the factories they open, of all those set speeches. . . If they cut down on these activities, the country would, after an initial culture-shock, come to appreciate a Ministerial speech as an event of some importance. The paradox of Irish political life is that Ministers are accorded far more respect (not least in the civil service)[48] than in many other European countries while being far more available to the public than elsewhere. I refuse to accept that there is a logical connection between these two factors!

Our electoral system (STV, multi-member constituencies) has added to the work-load of Ministers through the clientelism factor. If alternative PR systems which would diminish this factor, based for example on single member constituencies, are not introduced, we should seek to diminish clientelism by (a) providing State funding for a widespread system of Citizens Advice Bureaux and increased facilities for the Ombudsman and (b) seeking to ensure, by convention if possible, by legislation if necessary, that Parliamentary representations on behalf of individuals would be considered only after relief had been sought through these channels. Clientelism would also be reduced — at least at the centre — if more power were given to local government.

A reduction in the number of Departments and Ministers could well lead to a more efficient discharge of business by the Government, if only by reducing talk around the Cabinet table. There is no valid reason why administrative change and improvement should stop short at the door of the Cabinet chamber — and, for all I know perhaps, it has not in the years since I left the public service. The Government agenda often seemed to me to be over-crowded, to include many items which might sensibly have been dealt with otherwise — either by a more rigorous definition of items requiring Government approval or (in the case of more important items) by the use of Cabinet Committees. If, however, Cabinet Committees were to be used for this purpose, the ground rules and conventions would need to be spelt out *and observed,* since the record regarding the use of these Committees has, in general, been unsatisfactory. Apart from being overcrowded, the

Government agenda often included items backed up by documents of stupefying length (including, I must confess, submissions by the Minister for Finance on public expenditure) — all drafted, of course, by civil servants! The temptation to stop short at the obligatory summary must often have been overwhelming.

I have grave reservations as to whether public esteem for our system of Government is enhanced by the growing trend of publicising Cabinet business. We are now accustomed to being told that particular matters in the public eye will be, are being, and have been discussed in Cabinet. Frequently, Cabinet tensions are hinted at (particularly during Coalition Governments). The business of Government meetings is to announce *decisions,* not to titillate the public by the equivalent of 'what the butler saw' disclosures.

If there were fewer departments and fewer Ministers, if clientelism were reduced, if the Cabinet agenda were pruned, if Cabinet Committees were active and efficient, if submissions to Cabinet were short and sharp, then I have no doubt that the business of Government and of public administration would be run more efficiently. We could of course, hardly aspire to the example of Gladstone who was able, at times, to put off holding cabinet meetings for as long as three months! (Henderson, 1984, 86).

THE WORK OF PARLIAMENT

The tentacles of change must reach beyond the Government and into the Dáil and Seanad. It would be interesting — and salutary — to list the *significant* procedural changes made by both Houses since the early 1920s. Not many would accept that procedures are notably more efficient now than when the State was established. Efficiency is not, of course, the only criterion; the essentials of parliamentary democracy must be protected and nurtured. Parliament can, however, be brought into disrepute if its procedures and proceedings are archaic, cumbrous, and manifestly wasteful of time and effort. The procedure for parliamentary questions is a case in point. If the minutiae of local affairs have to be catered for — and why not, within limits — then written replies should be the norm, and oral replies an occasion of some significance. The debate on the Budget is another case in point — seemingly endless days of prolonged, discursive, open-to-all debates, with no holds barred. Is it asking too much that the party system which dominates politics should so organise affairs that the issues to be debated would be filtered through the party machine and expressed through a handful of deputies — to be varied from time to time, to give backbenchers a chance to show their paces?

Parliamentary committees are another — and my final — case in point. In less than a decade or so, we have moved from a situation in which there were just a handful of committees, most of which were concerned with the efficient running of the Oireachtas (to use the IPA terminology) to the present position where we have fifteen committees, of which ten deal with 'public business', to use Eunan O'Halpin's phrase. According to the IPA Yearbook 1987, these Oireachtas Committees had produced 81 reports in the lifetime of the 24th Dáil — up to August 1986. It is probably reasonable to regard the reports — thirty-one in all — produced by the Joint Committee on the Secondary Legislation of the European Communities as being in a special category. This still leaves fifty reports in less than four years from the other committees. While one can admire the zeal of these committees, a nagging doubt remains about the end-result of their labours. Preparation of the reports involved a major draw on the time of parliamentarians and civil servants. Substantial moneys were paid to consultants. But did all this substantial amount of time and money yield comparable results? The test to apply is not the interim one of reports produced but the more stringent one of *action* taken on foot of the reports. The parliamentarians may retort that action is not within their control — but to what extent has action at least been pressed for in Dáil and Seanad? In any event would it not be sensible to call a halt to more reports until either existing reports have been disposed of, or at least some understanding reached about the number of reports which can sensibly be absorbed by Parliament and administration within the lifetime of a Dáil? This is, no doubt, baying at the moon, though I am fortified in my view by Eunan O'Halpin's conclusion that 'experience would suggest that there are too many committees at present. . . there are sharp limits to the number that the Oireachtas can operate satisfactorily' (O'Halpin, 1986). The 25th Dáil will probably be as 'fruitful' in this respect as its predecessor and we can look forward to a mountain of reports, and very little action.

ADVISORY BODIES

Oireachtas reports are not unique in this respect. Irish Governments have a poor record for taking action on the reports of advisory bodies which they have established. It would be easier to list the reports on which action has been taken (including reasoned decisions for *not* adopting the report's recommendations) than it would be to enumerate those which have been, in effect, ignored by extensive and indeterminate delay. A moratorium should be called on such advisory reports for, say, five years. They cost too much, not alone in time and effort but also in the excuse they provide for not taking action. We have had enough paralysis by analysis.

My plea for a moratorium on reports does not spring from a belief that outsider advice is not required. Let us, however, accept that for a while we have enough of a good thing; let us give ourselves time to examine the advice we have received and to take whatever action is appropriate. It is salutary to bear in mind the Iron Law of Administration — action takes longer than you think. This applies even in regard to reports issued by the Government itself. Many of the recommendations in the admirable White Paper, *A Better Way to Plan the Nation's Finances* (PL299), have not yet been implemented although the White Paper was published over five years ago (November 1981). A more recent example is the White Paper on the Public Service — *Serving the Country Better* (PL3262) published in September 1985. This was described as 'a statement of decisions taken and a firm action plan. The necessary legislation be introduced immediately. . . .' (Paragraph 9.1). Although the Government had already approved the general lines of the necessary legislation (paragraph 9.6) the legislation was not enacted, nor was it even introduced, in the sixteen months which elapsed between the publication of the White Paper and the dissolution of the 24th Dáil. It is, perhaps, symptomatic of the point I am making that in the beginning of 1986, when the Public Service portfolio changed hands, the new Minister said that his predecessor had virtually completed the work of civil service reform. In fact it was just beginning.

There are many who will blame the civil service for the failure to implement, or for the delay in implementing, the findings and recommendations of parliamentary and advisory bodies, or to give effect to Governmental White Papers. This seems too facile a judgment, and, if blame has to be apportioned, it should not be hung around the neck of the civil service alone. In any event, the priority now should be to dam the rising flood of reports and to concentrate on action, not writing.

The press has an important part to play in securing better government — if only by keeping politicians and public servants on their toes. The press would, no doubt, claim that it could discharge its responsibilities more effectively but for the operation of the Official Secrets Acts — an issue which is outside the scope of this article. Given the reticence of public servants regarding publicity, (their aversion, in Mencken's phrase, to 'flapping their wings in public') the press does a good job in reporting on public administration — but I suggest that it might do much better if it applied more resources to the task. True, there are special correspondents for specific aspects of public administration, eg environment, diplomacy, security, but a general overview is lacking. I am reminded of the need for improvement whenever I read press comments about impending changes at the top of the public service. I would criticise the press, not for not knowing the individuals involved, but for the impressionistic inaccurate 'copy' they feel compelled to publish. Hardly a major issue, I agree, except possibly to the individuals concerned and to their bruised reputations.

In the last decade or so, outsider criticism of the Government's economic policies has been impressive whether reckoned in terms of volume, scope or sophistication. I would like to see corresponding progress in the area of public administration, in place of the unfounded generalisation which so often passes for comment on the public service. I accept that progress will require more openness from the service. Who will make the first move?

[March 1987]

11

Recollections

The literature on government and public administration in Ireland is sparse; sparser still is the contribution from within the public service. There are few biographies of Government Ministers — certainly few in which the role of the subject as Minister is predominant. With the exception of Dr Noel Browne, no Minister has published his or her autobiography — Earnán De Blaghd's memoirs, *Trasna na Bóinne, Slán le Últaibh* and *Gaeil Á Muscailt* can hardly be counted as they refer to his pre-ministerial career. At the time of writing Garret FitzGerald's memoirs and Gemma Hussey's cabinet diaries are awaited with understandable interest. The contribution from, or about, public servants is, if anything, sparser still. There are, for example, Leon Ó Broin's biography of Joseph Brennan *(No Man's Man,* Institute of Public Administration 1982) and his own autobiography *(Just Like Yesterday,* Gill & Macmillan 1986) but the life and work of the public servant is not the *raison d'être* of either book.

The scarcity of books by public servants on the public service is understandable. Most of a public servant's work will already be in the public domain, and, leaving aside tittle-tattle, he can add little, without breaching official secrecy, to what is already public knowledge. This broad statement should of course be qualified with one or other of the limiting phrases so popular in the public service — 'generally speaking', 'in most cases', etc. In individual cases, the urge to go public may well depend on the individual's self-esteem, the importance or otherwise of the areas in which he worked, his respect/disrespect for the Official Secrets Act or, more probably, by the frailty or otherwise of his memory. Few public servants keep private diaries of public affairs; the late Peter Berry, Secretary of the Department of Justice, was a well-known exception (see *Magill* May – June 1980; incidentally, I do not agree with some of his references to myself).

Insofar as a public servant's memoirs relate to his official life, the acid test is whether he has anything useful or interesting to add to what is already known about the public affairs in which he was involved.

In view of all these caveats, no one will be surprised when I disclaim any intention of writing an autobiographical memoir. The scope of this essay is much more modest, and is adequately described by its title — 'Recollections'. My recollections will bear on matters in the public domain, some relating to matters to which I was close, others not. Like many recollections, they will be somewhat disjointed. They will also be incomplete in the sense that they will not touch (or at least are not *intended* to touch) on aspects of the public service already covered by the other articles in this book. In particular, I will not discuss such issues as the need for change in the public service and the form which such change might take; I have nothing to add to my earlier views on these and related matters.

I joined the Civil Service in 1934; I was a reluctant civil servant, inasmuch as my first choice of career was medicine, and I had in fact attended some 'pre-medicine' lectures before it became clear to me that family circumstances ruled out a university-based career.

I spent nearly forty-two years in the Civil Service, and served in the Revenue Commissioners (14 years) the Departments of Agriculture (1 + years), the Taoiseach (8 years) and Finance (17 + years). My last seven years were spent as Secretary of the Department of Finance. I spent a further five-and-a-half years in the public service as Governor of the Central Bank of Ireland, retiring in 1981. I was a Director of the Northern Bank from 1982 to 1988, and Chairman of what became the National Irish Bank from 1986 to 1989.

My years in the Civil Service were neither all peaks nor all valleys. I recall with pride and pleasure my work for, and with, two Taoisigh — Eamon de Valera and John A. Costello — and their many acts of kindness and consideration. It was exhilarating to be involved in the preparation of *Economic*

Development and doubly so to be responsible (with Louden Ryan) for the work of the Economic Development Branch which pushed forward the frontiers of the Department of Finance. My promotion to Assistant (now Second) Secretary in that Department, and my assumption of responsibility for the newly-created Development Division, meant that the EDB *as such* had a relatively short life. This was a pity, since its work was novel, interesting, and beginning to bear fruit. There is, I suggest, need for some research into the EDB to see whether there are any lessons to be drawn, in 1990, from the approach adopted some thirty years ago.

ECONOMIC PLANNING

It is undeniable that Ireland adopted economic planning with all the fervour of the convert, and oversold the benefits of the new religion. *Post hoc, ergo propter hoc* became the order of the day. A sense of historical perspective, we are now told, 'would have encouraged greater modesty about the achievements of the 1960s by recognising that they depended heavily on a combination of uniquely favourable external/ internal circumstances' (Kennedy, Giblin, McHugh, 1988). But there is a considerable element of jobbing backwards in this criticism. The other side of the coin is the vital contribution which economic planning made to dispelling the deep depression of the mid- to late fifties — a depression which was in danger of becoming ingrained in the national psyche.

A central element in the earlier economic plans was the forecast capital budgets. The Government's enthusiasm for planning was not carried to the extreme of regarding these forecasts as binding — even with a modest allowance for contingencies. A cynic might have been tempted to ask how the public could be expected to take the plans seriously when the Government failed to take seriously that part of the plans which applied uniquely to it.

Since the *First Programme for Economic Expansion* was published in 1958, its successors have, in the words of the cliché, been 'too numerous to mention'. It would, I suggest, be a sobering and a shattering experience to list all the economic planning documents issued by the Government, the National Economic and Social Council and the National Planning Board in the last thirty years. Would it be too harsh a verdict to say that, if they were laid end to end, they would not arrive at a conclusion? Familiarity is in danger of breeding, if not contempt, at least irritation — institutional representatives are now tending to complain at not being given a 'credit' in the documents!

DEPARTMENT OF FINANCE

Looking back over the period following my appointment as Secretary to the Department of Finance (March 1969), a number of developments stand out in my mind. I had earlier noticed that it was normal to have more opportunities (e.g. at OECD functions) of meeting our English counterparts than our Northern Ireland ones. I made it my business, therefore, to establish contact with the Permanent Secretary to the Ministry of Finance in Belfast, and went north to meet him and some of his colleagues; I was surprised — perhaps I shouldn't have been — when I was brought in to meet Mr Brian Faulkner, then Prime Minister of Northern Ireland. The outbreak of the 'troubles' cut short that interchange, and although contact between the two Departments was resumed in the context of Sunningdale and of the power-sharing Executive, it was not quite the same thing.

An early by-product of the 'troubles' was, of course, the NI Grant-in-Aid 1969/70, the Arms Trial and the special examination by the Public Accounts Committee of the Grant-in-Aid. I was involved in that examination in my capacity as Accounting Officer of the Department rather than as an active participant in the disbursement of the Grant-in-Aid (which I was not). The affair (if I might call it that) is an example of the all-embracing responsibilities of an Accounting Officer. Indeed one of the by-products of the affair was that I took care to step down as Accounting Officer of a number of Votes (e.g. the Department of the Taoiseach, Houses of the Oireachtas and others) which, by custom and default in the past, had fallen on the shoulders of the Secretary of the Department of Finance.

A third development in those early years was the decision to ask Ronan Fanning (now Professor) to write a history of the Department. I am grateful to the late George Colley, then Minister for Finance, and to Richie Ryan, his successor, for agreeing so readily to my suggestion. It was an illuminating experience to watch a professional historian at work on the mass of papers involved, and to see how he imposed order on the inchoate material. There is common agreement that the book was an objective and valuable contribution to the history, not alone of Ireland, but also of public administration in Ireland. Although the book was not published until 1978, two years after I left the Department; I kept in touch with it until completion.

As Fanning mentions in the Preface, his brief was to pay 'particular attention to the Department's origins and early years'. The object was to draw attention to the administrative difficulties involved in the transition from dependence to independence, and to the problems of building an Irish financial administration on the foundations inherited from the British. Our founding fathers have been criticised for not adopting a different administrative model, but such criticism overlooks the essentially conservative nature of the movement which gave us independence (Farrell, 1988). It is fashionable now in certain quarters to deride the progress we have made in the past seventy years or so, and to underline how much we have fallen behind other Western European countries. We are told that our only distinguishing marks are backwardness and dirt, that we are the stunted bonhams of Europe — or that (to change the metaphor) we have relegated ourselves from First Division status pre-independence to Third Division status nowadays. For a more sober — though still chastening — assessment of how we have fared, we must turn to the measured words of the economists. It seems that there is 'some doubt about whether Ireland was as well-off relatively, in 1913, as the figures suggest' and in any event 'this (1913) position was attained, however, in an unusual way — through massive population decline with a very low growth of total output'. We have to accept, however, that 'Ireland's achievements since independence translate into a very mediocre record compared with the generality of European countries' (Kennedy, Giblin, McHugh, 1988). This is a far cry from First Division/Third Division stuff.

If we are looking backward, we should not ignore the enormous improvements we have achieved in living standards since we attained independence. Living standards 'are about three times higher on average than in the 1920s' *(ibid)*. Of course not all the indicators point in the same direction (emigration and unemployment are obvious examples) but the overall trend is unmistakable and positive, even when account is taken of the rise in the National Debt. Perhaps Yeats may not have been right in the words he attributed to Parnell:

> Parnell came down the road, he said to a cheering man;
> 'Ireland shall get her freedom and you still break stone.'

Another development which I recall in the years following my appointment as Secretary of the Department of Finance was the emergence of formal deficit budgeting in 1972. I use the word 'formal' because there were, of course, devices in operation prior to that year which helped *ex ante* to avoid a formal deficit; global deductions were made from expenditure on Supply Services in recognition of a general overestimation by Departments and, from time to time, items previously classified as current were reclassified as capital.

Given that the circumstances of 1972 required the Government to give a boost to the economy, it could be argued that this should have taken the form of increasing public capital spending. But increasing the Capital Budget at relatively short notice can run up against the problem of finding worthwhile projects, and there were already enough dubious projects in that Budget.

The theoretical justification for unbalanced budgets (whether in surplus or in deficit) had been mentioned in the Minister's Supplementary Budget of autumn 1970 and was referred to in the 1972 Budget. What was not foreseen, however, was a political factor which has little to do with the economic theories of deficit budgeting. I refer to the reluctance of politicians to accept the cyclical adjustments required by a policy of deficit budgeting. In principle, lip service was paid to the need to eliminate the deficit in X years time (X being a variable feast). In practice, the current budget deficit, which in 1972 was a tiny percentage of GNP, has been with us ever since. For many years it was a significant percentage of GNP; the substantial reduction in the last two years was the result of serendipy rather than of deliberate policy. We have come to take for granted the inflated services made possible by deficit budgeting, while protesting even at the taxes *needed to prevent the deficits from increasing.* Of course the world would be rosy if all the tax arrears were collected, if the tax net were spread more widely... But would the deficits disappear? We came close to fiscal virtue in 1990 when the *opening* Budgetary position was, effectively, in surplus (£24 million), but the customary handouts transformed this into a projected deficit of £261 million.

While I agree with the emphasis currently placed on the need to stabilise the National Debt/GNP ratio, I think that stabilisation/reduction in the ratio should be achieved by steady and progressive reductions in the current budget deficit rather than in the Capital Budget. The sophistication of the argument relating to the National Debt/GNP ratio (and here may I acknowledge the high standard of economic analysis nowadays) should not divert attention from the social, political — even moral — issues posed by an almost *indefinite* reliance on current budget deficits.

As one who has criticised the profligate increase in the National Debt, may I say how shocked I am at the suggestion that we should now repudiate that Debt. I find such a suggestion morally repugnant and most dangerous for our self-esteem. Even assessed coldly and narrowly in economic terms, repudiation would damage severely (probably fatally) a host of institutions (banks, insurance companies, pension funds etc) which feature Government stock prominently in their balance sheets, while facing with ruin many thousands of individual holders of worthless Government Stock, Saving Certificates, Savings Bonds etc. Of course it may be argued (although in fact it has *not* been) that what is in mind is selective repudiation e.g. of external National Debt — good enough for the misguided foreigners who our word for our bond.

THE SYSTEM OF PROMOTION

Hierarchy is the hallmark of a bureaucracy such as the Civil Service, and promotion, as the means of moving up in the hierarchy, is never far from a civil servant's mind. A good promotional system is essential for the well-being of the organisation and for the satisfaction of the individual. The problems posed become particularly acute when promotions at and above a particular grade — say Principal Officer — are involved. This is not to say that great care and consideration are not required in the case of promotions at lower level but, because of the greater responsibilities involved and the possibility of further advancement to the highest level, promotions to Principal Officer posts and above require and receive particular attention from top management. I can testify to the attention which these promotions received in the Department of Finance. The guiding principle was no problem — promotion should be on merit. It was the application of the principle which was often the difficulty. Sometimes, of course, there was no dispute or disagreement about the winner, either at top level or generally within the Department. But disputes there were; either top level opinion was initially not unanimous, or the verdict was received with quite mixed feelings in the Department. In large part the problem stemmed from the difficulty of devising objective indicators of merit and of implementing genuine (as distinct from nominal) assessment procedures. At the heart of the problem was the issue of reconciling what was best for the Department with justice for the individual or, more precisely, of establishing procedures which would satisfy the man passed over that he had been given a fair crack of the whip (an unfortunate metaphor).

It was in this sense that, as I say, top level promotions caused me, at least, particular difficulty. And let me hasten to add that this *post-factum* heart-searching is not intended to cast the slightest aspersion on those who were in fact promoted. Perhaps things are better ordered now. For posts at Assistant Secretary and Secretary level, there is now in place a system of inter-departmental competition, the Top Level Appointments Committee.

I was fortunate to have served in a number of Government

Departments and Offices. One of the benefits of the TLAC system is that it facilitates this inter-departmental exchange. To the outsider the civil service appears as a monolith; to the insider it is more often than not a series of quasi-independent republics. Any development which helps to build bridges between these republics is welcome and worthwhile.

DEPARTMENT OF THE TAOISEACH

When the State was established, the number of Departments was eleven. That number has since increased to seventeen, typically by sub-division of existing Departments e.g. the 'old' Department of Industry and Commerce has fathered the present Department of Industry and Commerce, the Department of Labour, the Department of Energy and the Department of Tourism and Transport. The former Department of Local Government and Public Health has fathered the Department of the Environment, the Department of Health and the Department of Social Welfare. Simply to list the number of new Departments created and the occasional Department suppressed would be to miss out on what, in my view, was the most significant Departmental change since the establishment of the State. I refer to the increase in size and importance of the Department of the Taoiseach.

For many decades after its establishment, this Department was small but high-powered. Apart from a handful of support staff, it consisted (with occasional variations) of a Secretary, Assistant Secretary, Principal Officer and Assistant Principal Officer. Its functions were, in Maurice Moynihan's words, 'to give to the Taoiseach and to the Government that necessary secretarial assistance in carrying out the important and arduous work that they are called upon to do' (Moynihan, 1960). This (typically) modest description involved, we may be sure, far more than the observer of the British scene had in mind when he wrote:

The Cabinet rises and goes to its dinner
The Secretary stays and gets thinner and thinner

Scratching his brains to record and report.
What he thinks that they think that they ought to have
thought
(Bruce-Gardyne, 1980).

It was not until the 1970s that any significant increase in higher-level staff took place. The total in 1979 came to eleven. By the end of 1989 the total in the 'inner' Department at HEO level and upwards was close to forty (ten times the traditional number) while the total staff (Secretariat, Government Information Service, Public Record Office, National Museum, National Library, National Gallery, etc.) was well over three hundred. The increase in staff reflects additional (but often unspecified) functions taken on, and expansion of traditional functions, to such an extent that we have now virtually a new Department — and one which (I suggest) poses a number of issues.

Is the development symptomatic of a tendency towards Prime Ministerial style Government? Has the vastly increased Department added to, or subtracted from, the overall efficiency of public administration? Would it be better if the work of the Government Secretariat and the Office of the Taoiseach were formally separated? Should the Taoiseach be burdened with the responsibility for such functions as the National Library, the National Museum, the National Gallery ...? Is there a danger that (to borrow an American phrase) 'there are too many people trying to bite you with the President's teeth?' (Rose and Suleiman, 1982). Even allowing for the fact that informed public comment on public administration is rare, I am surprised that these issues have not received some airing. They touch on an important area of politics and public administration. What was said about Whitehall is true about Merrion Street: 'In the nervous system of Whitehall, the Prime Minister's Office is the ganglion'.[49]

INDEPENDENCE OF THE CIVIL SERVICE

The independence of the civil service — independence to proffer the advice which it considers best in the public interest — should never be taken for granted. The best safeguard of this independence is peer assessment, although I can appreciate the viewpoint of those who maintain that official secrecy should be relaxed to enable the public to judge the soundness and independence of the advice proffered to Ministers. The views of a former public servant on official secrecy will hardly be regarded as objective and impartial. Let me, nevertheless, go on the record as favouring some - indeed a considerable - dilution of the present catch-all embargo, but as being sceptical of the many advantages which some foresee in the change; I know of one foreign institution which was required, by law, to publish the minutes of its Board Meetings, but which lived happily by having *two* types of Board Meetings - an informal one and a formal one. An administrative version of Gresham's Law?

Whether it comes through a relaxation of the Official Secrets Acts or through changes resulting from the work of the Ombudsman, I am convinced that more information about his or her individual case should be available to the citizen affected by Government action or inaction in relation to social welfare benefits, taxation, etc. I would be inclined to go more slowly regarding disclosure relating to major policy issues, and have reservations — to put it mildly - about calls by the media for such disclosure. My reservations stem in part from what I regard as the deplorable record of the press in regard to leaked information. I have known cases where the press printed leaked versions of *draft* reports. Their record reminds me - unfairly, I admit - of what was said in another context about the British press:

> You cannot hope to bribe or twist
> Thank God! the British journalist
> But, seeing what the man will do
> Unbribed, there's no occasion to.

It would be a mistake to link the independence of the civil

service with pay - at least unless and until matters got entirely out of hand, resulting in moonlighting, widespread bribery, etc. On civil service pay I will content myself with just two observations — one substantial, one trivial. My experience since I left the civil service has confirmed my suspicion that pay at the top of the civil service is seriously out of line with that for jobs with somewhat comparable responsibility in the private sector. For good or evil, top civil service pay is linked both in amount and in timing with Ministerial pay. Adjustments of Ministerial pay are usually delayed and inadequate — not because of an inferiority complex, but because adjustments are regarded as hot political potatoes. So top civil service (and Ministerial) pay lags and lurches far behind the going rate in the private sector.

My trivial point relates to the fine tuning of civil service pay. This arises from the application of percentage increases, and the refusal to engage in rounding-off, no matter how modestly. Thus we end up with the position where, for example, the pay of a general service Assistant Secretary ranges from £31,851 to £35,567 - can precision go further than this?

THE WORK OF THE DÁIL

In reviewing the number of Deputies as provided for in the Constitution, we have tended to opt for the maximum number permitted under the Constitution; incidentally this is yet another example of the 'fussiness' of our Constitution - it is legislation, rather than the Constitution, which should govern the minimum and maximum number of parliamentary representatives. It is a moot point whether even the minimum number of representatives provided by the Constitution would be excessive for our needs; there is a number of conflicting considerations to be taken into account, and international comparisons can be misleading. It would be difficult, however, to argue that we need more parliamentary representatives and I think that it would not be out of place if, on the next review, the maximum provision was modified, even if slightly.

Of far more importance, however, is whether we are making the best use of our parliamentary representatives. This turns on the way in which the Dáil is run (the Seanad is of course also relevant, but is another day's work). There has been a number of developments in the last decade or so, designed to make the Dáil more effective. There are, for example, many more Dáil Committees than heretofore – but it is doubtful if there has been a commensurate increase in the effectiveness of the Dáil, even on a quite broad definition of effectiveness. Part of the problem lies in the lack of consistent and effective follow-up procedures. Leaving the committee system aside, it is doubtful whether a parliamentary Rip Van Winkle, who was familiar with the Dáil procedures of 1922, would discern any major changes in the Dáil procedures of 1989. The Dáil still operates on the eighteenth century convention of parliament as a debating chamber in which oratory moulds and changes opinions and votes. Oratory has, of course, long since departed, but the convention, although displaced by a rigid party system, still gives every deputy the right to speak. Hence the extended 'debates' on most Bills and Motions, during which the law of diminishing returns rarely fails to operate. If we have a party system, why should the parties not control the debates, presenting party views through one or two spokespersons? Spokespersons could be changed according to the subject matter at issue.

It could of course be argued that this would be unfair to some back-benchers who have little enough chance to bring themselves to public attention – indeed I could be accused of not recognising that the Dáil system works only because back-benchers can let off steam during debates. Maybe so, but parliamentary democracy surely requires a more up-to-date, honest, and effective approach.

Time saved on Dáil debates is valuable only if it is put to good use. An obvious candidate is the follow-up to the work of Dáil committees.

The more attention is focused on the work of the Dáil (and Seanad), the more relevant becomes the issue of the appropriate pay of parliamentarians. First we have to decide whether membership of Parliament should be a full-time career. Our present approach seems undecided, if not ambiguous, on this issue, but the pay involved is hardly consistent with parliamentarians being engaged full-time. It is easy to fall into circular argument here - pay being related to the value placed on parliamentary work, but parliamentary work being undervalued because pay is not sufficient to attract and obtain enough high-class people. There are of course many honourable exceptions, and also many people for whom power, not money, is the attraction.

I suspect that our approach to parliamentary pay reflects, if only in part, the nineteenth century belief that this work was the domain and prerogative of well-heeled gentlemen; we tend to forget that the payment of parliamentarians featured prominently in the early campaigns for the reform of parliament. Couple with this the low esteem in which politics and politicians are generally (but undeservedly) held, and it is not surprising that the question of increasing parliamentary pay is not high on the national agenda.

Whether or not we have too many parliamentary representatives (and, as I have said, we have given ourselves the maximum permitted by the Constitution) it is undeniable that it is difficult for the party in Government to find people of the right calibre from within its ranks to appoint as Ministers, and Ministers of State. Typically, that party will have eighty Deputies or less in the Dáil and will have to provide a Taoiseach, fourteen Ministers, and fifteen Ministers of State — a tough job, having regard to the number of members who don't want to serve, who can't be allowed to serve, or who are in the wrong constituencies. This factor adds force to the contention that we have too many Ministers. In part this is because we have too many Departments, although a few Ministers are in charge of more than one Department. It is worth recalling that it was not until 1973 that the Government reached the maximum number — fifteen — permitted by the Constitution. The problem has grown mainly because of the tendency to create new Departments in response to pressure for particular attention to be given to particular aspects of a Department's work. This is a process without end; there are constant demands for yet more Departments, and it is probably true that we would have had more but for the constitutional limit on the number of Ministers (another example of

Constitutional 'fussiness') and the practical limit on the extent to which Ministers can double-up.

I maintain that we would be better served by having fewer rather than more Ministers. The calibre of Ministers would improve and, hopefully, what we would pay them would be more in keeping with the importance of their work. But how could fewer Ministers deal with the existing ministerial workload? In part, I would suggest, by the new approach to parliamentary work as outlined above. In part by the adoption of the Aireacht principle, as recommended twenty years ago by the Devlin Group. In part, by a revision of our system of proportional representation which would reduce the clientelism which so clogs the Irish political machine, and, finally, by giving more power to district, local and regional authorities.

However desirable some of these suggestions may be in their own right, it is possible that only a more fundamental reshaping of our system of parliament and of government will enable us to cope adequately with the public workload of the last quarter of the twentieth century. Perhaps we need something on the lines of a legal separation of executive and parliament, as advocated by John Roden, Donal de Buitleir and Donal O'Brolchain in 'A Design for Democracy'.[50] It is a pity that their interesting suggestions have not stimulated a debate, whether of refutation or endorsement.

THE PUBLIC SECTOR-PRIVATE SECTOR SYNDROME

We hear less nowadays of the assertion that public affairs should be managed on the same lines as private business — although the prescription is still occasionally given an airing. Public servants have to be careful that, in rebutting the assertion, they do not inadvertently give the impression that efficiency is either irrelevant or satisfactory in the public sector. But those who prescribe private sector efficiency as the remedy for public sector ills are demonstrating that they know little or nothing about the objectives and constraints of the public sector. I wonder is Ireland unique in the distance that is maintained between the two sectors? There are, of course, many contacts at individual level (hardly surprising given how small the country is) and attempts have been made (with pathetically limited success) to interchange personnel between the two sectors. Yet each sector can and does complain that the other sector does not understand it and has a distorted and often hostile view of its activities. There are, no doubt, some in the private sector who would apply the Australian term 'Government stroke' to the Irish public sector. Derived from convict times, the Government stroke was the convict's irreducible unit of labour; 'Doing it kept you out of the hands of the flogger. You were seen to be working but that was all' (Hughes, 1987).

It is many years since Ivor Kenny identified the stereotyped images which each sector has of the other. I remember at the time thinking that the private sector viewpoint could be expressed in lines borrowed and adapted from those of a 19th century English divine:

I thank the goodness and the grace
which on my birth have smiled
To make me in these days of stress,
a happy private sector child.

I cannot say whether adoption of the current suggestion to bring together the management training activities of the Institute of Public Administration and the Irish Management Institute would help to bridge the gap in understanding. It is ironical that a fusion of the two Institutes was proposed over twenty-five years ago by the IPA - and rejected by the IMI.

Incidentally, anyone who wishes to get a feel of how differently things are done in the two sectors need only look at these two Institutes. Both Institutes have been financially supported, directly and indirectly, by the Exchequer. As its activities expanded, the IMI has been able to relocate itself in a spacious, purpose-built building, while the IPA has had to be content with temporary buildings, learning the bitter truth of the French saying that it is only the provisional which lasts.

When it comes to frugality, the civil service is often hardest on itself. In the past, the standard of civil service accommodation was often disgraceful and frequently in breach of the

Offices Acts. It took a combination of trade union pressure and the need to improve public reception areas to effect much needed changes. Let me give a trivial example to illustrate my general point. When I became Secretary of the Department of Finance I found that at some stage in the past an allowance had been provided for Departmental Secretaries to cover entertainment costs which could not easily be vouched (and therefore could not otherwise be recouped). The amount involved, per Secretary, was £100 per annum (as I said, the example is trivial). I thought that, with the passage of time, it would be appropriate to increase the allowance but, over-fearful of leaving the senior civil service open to the charge of self-aggrandisement, I mentioned the suggestion to the then Minister - who turned it down!

There are, of course, other examples of public service frugality imposed on the public sector. The fees payable to Board members of state-sponsored bodies are a case in point. In the case of the older bodies, the fees may originally have borne some relationship to those payable in the private sector; by this I mean that they may, for example, have been one-half of the going private sector rate. With the passage of time, with the steady increase in private sector fees and with the reluctance to increase public sector fees ('there never is a right time . . .') the fees typically paid by State bodies are but a small fraction of those paid in the private sector. In some cases, where reasonably exact comparisons can be made, the discrepancy is ludicrous.

Of course it may be argued that people serve on these bodies not because of the fee they receive but out of a sense of public duty (there may be other, less commendable, motives). Fair enough, but the fees were not initially based on that assumption, and what we have at the moment is the result of inertia and of reluctance to move with the times. There are, of course, exceptions. In the case of the B + I, economic necessity forced a by-passing of the Devlin guidelines. In the case of Telecom Eireann, Dr. Smurfit (its Chairman) recounts that he insisted on '... the highest paid chairmanship of the semi-states. . . I wanted to establish that the Board would be professional, not political' (Kenny, 1987). He cannot have been too happy with the report of the Ombudsman for 1987 which showed that, in that year, the complaints against Telecom Eireann exceeded the complaints received against the *entire* civil service.

It would, of course, be difficult to establish a causal relationship between the amount of fees paid and the quality of Board membership, since so many members were appointed on political grounds, and were not re-appointed, also on political grounds. Even when not appointed on political grounds, some board members have found that it was political considerations (e.g. a change of Government) which were responsible for their not being re-appointed. At times, indeed, the decision not to re-appoint was tardily conveyed. I recall the case of a Chairman who travelled from a provincial town to the Annual General Meeting of his State company in Dublin, only to find on arrival that he was no longer Chairman. The treatment of Joseph Brennan was no better. On 14th March 1953, he tendered his resignation as Governor of the Central Bank, the resignation to take effect 'from an early date'. On the 31st March he heard that his resignation had been accepted, effective from 1st April - and later received the Taoiseach's letter of 31st March to that effect (Moynihan, 1975).

Somewhat different is the fate of those who respond to a call by the Government to act on a Commission/Committee to examine and report on a particular problem. Here I am thinking not so much of those who represent sectional interests on the Commission/Committee as of the 'independent members' and in particular of the Chairman. These usually put in an enormous amount of unpaid work — often to no avail. The old gibe, that the establishment of such a Commission/Committee is but an excuse to defer action, has many, many, germs of truth in it. It would be tedious, and hardly worthwhile, to try to establish statistically the truth of this, but I would be amazed if more than one in five such bodies had a significant part of their recommendations adopted within even ten years of reporting. Of course, maybe some reports were worthless — but nearly all of them?

MINISTERS AND OTHERS

In his Foreword to Fanning's book, the late George Colley, then Tánaiste and Minister for Finance, drew attention to 'the fact that politicians are not required to commit their thoughts to paper to the same degree as civil servants'. I doubt whether this factor alone explains the dearth of published political memoirs. Whatever the explanation, I can recall only one Ministerial autobiography - *Against the Tide,* by Noel Browne. The coverage of his Ministerial career, while significant, takes up only a relatively small part of the book. It is ironic that in a country so devoid of public sector literature, we should have two other books on the period and area covered by Dr Browne's Ministerial career - those by Ruth Barrington and James Deeney (Barrington, 1987, Deeney, 1989). These serve as a useful counterweight to the rather egotistical account of his stewardship given by Dr Noel Browne. But perhaps the most telling comment is to be found in Dr Brendan Hensey's factual and objective history of the health services; in dealing with the period covered by Dr Browne's Ministry, he concludes pointedly that 'The tide was flowing with him'. (Hensey, 1988).

Dr Browne speaks well of few of his fellow politicians, and bitterly and bitingly about many of them. It is only right to recall, therefore, that he speaks highly of his Department.

Dr Deeney's autobiography provides one of the rare glimpses of Ministers as seen by their civil servants. Of Dr Browne he says that he 'seemed to be patently sincere, had great energy, an attractive personality' but, before their ways parted, he summed him up as 'ruthless, and much more calculating than people thought and possibly indeed vindictive'. Here was, indeed, a clash of personalities!

It used to be a familiar gibe of the media that Ministers were 'birds of passage'. It is undeniable that many Ministers have relatively short tenures of their Departments. The average life of postwar Governments is not much more than three years; few Ministers serve in successive Governments in the same Departments. Leon O'Broin recalls that in his twenty years in the Department of Posts and Telegraphs he served under ten Ministers; in my seventeen years in Finance I served under five Ministers. At times of short-lived Governments one tends to recall that the original Monsieur Silhouette was a French Minister for Finance under Louis XV.

If we are to believe Dr James Deeney, the priority of a Secretary of a Department is to please his Minister. While I would never have recognised myself in that description, it is undeniable that the public concerns of a Minister are the concerns of his Departmental Secretary. This official lives very much in the eye of the storm, where the day-today pressure is intense and where the urgent takes precedence over the important. This became pleasantly obvious to me when I moved over to the Central Bank — as compared with being unpleasantly obvious in the preceding decade. As the Devlin Group recognised some twenty years ago, this overwhelming pressure on Ministers and senior civil servants can be eased only by a radical restructuring of the civil service; the vexed question of the last two decades is why this restructuring has not taken place. Hope flared anew with the publication of the 1985 White Paper, *Serving the Country Better,* but has died down again over the last four years or so. There are those who point the finger at ministerial impotence and civil service indifference; others lay the blame on ministerial indifference and civil service impotence.

In another context, Arthur Koestler called for the establishment of an active fraternity of pessimists:

> They will not aim at immediate radical solutions, because they know that these cannot be achieved in the hollow of the historical wave; they will not brandish the surgeon's knife at the social body, because they know that their own instruments are polluted. They will watch with open eyes and without sectarian blinkers for the first sight of the new horizontal movement; when it comes they will assist its birth; but if it does not come in their lifetime, they will not despair. And meantime their chief aim will be to create oases in the interregnum desert.[51]

Perhaps the cause of administrative reform in Ireland would best be served by an active fraternity of Irish pessimists.

[July 1989]

12

Notes to Chapters

1. In my own case, my intention to retire for personal reasons, before the end of my term of office, had been notified to the Minister for Finance before the General Election of June 1981, and confirmed after that election (author).
2. *Press Review of the Bank for International Settlements* 5 February 1980.
3. Arthur Burns in evidence to the House of Representatives Committee on Banking, Currency and Housing (Federal Reserve consultations on the conduct of monetary policy) 94th Congress, 2nd Session, July 1976, H 241-36.
4. Sir Theodore Gregory, The Stamp Memorial Lecture 1955.
5. Dáil Debates, 16 February 1971 Cols 1468/70. A statement on somewhat similar lines was made by the Minister for Finance in Seanad Éireann on the Second Reading of the Organisation for Economic Cooperation and Development (Financial Support Fund) (Agreement) Bill 1976 — *Seanad Éireann Debates* 30 June 1976.
6. Reproduced in *Press Review of the Bank for International Settlements* 20 October 1977. For a

different view of the autonomy of the Bundesbank, see 'Central Bank Behaviour; A positive empirical analysis' by Frey and Schneider *Journal of Monetary Economics* (1981) pp. 291-315: 'Over the period covered (1957 II through 1977 IV) there are seven (quarterly) time spans in which there was a conflict between the central bank and government. . . In the end the Bundesbank yielded to the pressure and undertook an expansionary monetary policy'.
7. Per Jacobsson Lecture, 9 November 1966.
8. For an excellent discussion of this subject, see the address on 'Raising Productivity in the Civil Service' given by Kevin Murphy, Deputy Secretary, Department of the Public Service, to the Institute of Personnel Management, 19 January 1982.
9. The British experience was similar; *vide* Garrett's comment that 'the optimists had over-estimated the capacity of a huge and long-established organisa-tion to change its ways, particularly when top manage-ment was not committed to change and the political will for

change was not maintained'. *Managing the Civil Service,* Heinemann, London 1980.

10. Cf. Kevin Murphy *op. cit.:* 'But the [Devlin] report was very complex and raised key political issues, two in particular. Were Ministers prepared to take their fingers out of every pie? Was the Dáil prepared to free large areas of Government administration from day-to-day control? We have not *yet* got answers to these two questions'.

11. *Report of the public service advisory council* (Appendix 2) Year ended 31 October 1980. According to the latest report — to October 1981 — the emphasis in the (reorganisation) programme has shifted from the purely structural towards the improvement of management processes generally.

12. Cf. Kevin Murphy *op. cit.:* 'The Department of the Public Service was, therefore, faced with the long haul of implementing the Devlin Report . . . Many managements, including a number of Ministers and Secretaries, were sceptical about the new structures and in some cases actively opposed to them. Others took the purely pragmatic approach of what was in it for them by way of extra staff.'

13. Dáil Debates Vol. 187 Col. 67, 7 March, 1961.

14. Quoted in *Ministers and their Mandarins* by Sir Douglas Allen (Government and Opposition, 1977, Vol. 12, No. 2).

15. Cf. Sir Edward Playfair (himself a permanent secretary of two British departments) '. . . all permanent Secretaries should be compulsorily retired after five years in the rank.' *Public Administration* Vol. 43, No. 3.

16. Brendan Walsh *The Sunday Press* 8 November 1981.

17. It was denied in a statement issued by the Minister for Finance, 23 July, 1973.

18. Thornley and Chubb 'Irish government observed' in *The Irish Times.*

19. Brendan Halligan *Hibernia* 6 July 1978.

20. *Irish Business* May 1977.

21. *Hibernia* 30 July 1976.

22. 'The government of change' address at the conferring of national diplomas in business studies, Regional Technical College, Dundalk 6 March 1980.

23. *Hibernia* 20/27 December 1979.

24. *Magill* December 1980.

25. Cf. Dr J. R. Dempsey, 'Administrative Reorganisation in Irish and American Contexts' *Administration,* Vol. 30, No. 1: '. . . the PSORG recommendations may have been too ambitious and perhaps too radical to have any real chance of immediate realisation'.

26. Policy for Economic Recovery, *Irish Times* 15 October 1982.

27. John Bruton, TD, 'The Issues', *Irish Times* 24 November 1982.

28. Fine Gael-Labour Programme for Government, *Irish Times* 13 December 1982.

29. *Irish Times* 4 February 1965, quoted in Bew and Patterson, *Seán Lemass and the making of modern Ireland, 1945/1966* Gill and Macmillan, 1982.

30. Richard Bruton, TD, *Irish Times* 25 January 1983.

31. This is not the only instance in which the administrative system

which we inherited from Britain differs from those elsewhere. The British system of Permanent (Departmental) Secretaries is rarely found in Mainland Europe — a factor not without significance for the issue of ministerial responsibility. Administrative law is a Continental, not British, concept. The role and status of the Treasury is rarely paralleled elsewhere in Europe. Different does not, of course, mean better.

32. Cf. *The Report of the Committee on Public Expenditure: Review of Department of the Public Service May 1985 (PL 3233):* 'The Committee consider that there is a certain duplication or, at least, a lack of clarity between particular activities undertaken by the Departments of Finance and the D.P.S.' (para. 85).

33. *Public Service Administrative Research Plan 1985-1990,* issued by the Department of the Public Service.

34. The need for research facilities *within* Departments is highlighted in a recent report on the Irish Wealth Tax (ESRI Research Paper No. 123: The Irish Wealth Tax: A Case Study in Economics and Politics, by Cedric Sandford and Oliver Morrissey). Having concluded that the Wealth Tax was a 'costly failure', the authors dryly pointed out (page 105) that 'If the Revenue had a research facility which anticipated necessary tax modifications, politicians might be saved from the more extreme pressures which are apt to lead to promises and actions which are hasty and ill-considered'.

35. *Annual Report of the Ombudsman.* Ireland 1984 (PI 2909).

36. A phrase I borrow (although the context is different) from Conor Cruise O'Brien's *The Suspecting Glance* (Faber and Faber 1972).

37. For a recent assessment of clientelism, see 'Class, Clientelism and the Political Process' by E. Hazelkorn in *Ireland, A Sociological Profile* (ed) P. Clancy et al., I.P.A. 1986.

38. *The Listener* 17 October 1985.

39. This suggestion was overtaken by events: the D.P.S. was dissolved early in 1987.

40. Civil Service Department, *The Civil Services of North America* HMSO 1969.

41. Ibid.

42. John Griffiths, 'Australian Administrative Law: Institutions, Reforms and Impact', *Public Administration* Vol 63 Winter 1985. See also L. J. Curtis 'The Australian Experience' in C. Burns op. cit.

43. Quoted in Hebbelwaite, Peter, *In The Vatican* Sedgewick and Jackson 1980.

44. The reply given to a parliamentary question on 28 October 1987 shows that eight of the Secretaries appointed under TLAC auspices were aged over 50 years on appointment, two were under 40 years and three were in their forties, the average age being about 51 years.

45. Brendan M. Walsh. Comment on Rose's 1986 study.

46. C.S. Lewis, 'Bulverism or the Foundation of Twentieth-Century Thought', in *First and Second Things,* Collins 1985.

47. Mansergh, Nicholas 1983, foreword to John McColgan,

British Policy and the Irish Administration, George Allen and Unwin. Liam de Paor takes a different view: '. . . the British withdrawal had left behind, like a constipating potion in the wells, the imperial civil service'. *The Peoples of Ireland,* Hutchinson 1986, p. 305.

48. Browne, Noel, *Against the Tide,* Gill and Macmillan, 1986. Dr Noel Browne, Minister for Health 1948/1951, who expressed surprise at being addressed as Minister by his civil servants, said that 'The word was hissed out with the kind of reverence which the Chinese reserve for their aged'.

49. Sampson, Anthony, *The Anatomy of Britain,* quoted in King, A. (ed) *The British Prime Minister* 2nd Edition, Macmillan, 1985.

50. *Administration* Vol. 34 No. 2. See also Ó Brolcháin, Donal, 'Ireland's Second Revolution — A View from the Future', *Seirbhís Phoiblí* Vol. 8 No. 2.

51. Quoted in Darby, John, *Conflict in Northern Ireland: The Development of a Planned Community,* Gill & Macmillan, 1976.

13

Bibliography

Abernach, Putnam and Rockman, *Bureaucrats and Politicians in Western Democracies,* Harvard University Press, 1981.

Acheson and Chant, 'Bureaucratic Theory and the Choice of Central Bank Goals', *Journal of Money Credit and Banking,* 1/2, May 1971.

Albrow, Martin, *Bureaucracy,* Pall Mall Press, London, 1970.

Armstrong, Sir William, *Role and Character of the Civil Service,* Oxford University Press, 1970.

Attlee, C.R., 'Civil Servants, Ministers, Parliament and the Public', *Political Quarterly,* Vol. 25, No. 4, 1954.

Balogh, T., 'The Apotheosis of the Dilettante' in Thomas, Hugh, ed, *Crisis in the Civil Service,* Anthony Blond, 1968.

Barnett, Joel, *Inside the Treasury,* Andre Deutsch, 1982.

Barrington, Ruth, *Health, Medicine and Politics in Ireland,* Institute of Public Administration, 1987.

Barrington, T.J., *The Irish Administrative System,* Institute of Public Administration, 1980.

Barrington, T.J., 'Whatever happened to Irish government?' in Litton, F., ed., *Unequal Achievement, The Irish Experience 1957-82,* Institute of Public Administration, 1982.

Barrington, T.J., 'The White Paper, Serving the Country Better. Serve You Right?', *Administration,* Vol. 33, No. 4, 1985.

Bridges, Sir Edward, *Portrait of a Profession: The Civil Service Tradition,* Cambridge University Press, 1953.

Brittan, Samuel, 'The Irregulars' in Rose, R., ed, *Policy Making in Britain,* Macmillan, 1969.

Browne, Noel, *Against the Tide,* Gill and Macmillan, 1986.

Bruce-Gardyne, Jock, *Ministers and Mandarins: Inside the Whitehall Village,* Sidgwick and Jackson 1980.

Brunner, Karl, 'The Case against Monetary Activism', *Lloyds Bank Review,* Jan. 1981.

Burns, C., ed, *The Path to Reform,* New Zealand Institute of Public Administration, 1982.

Chant and Acheson, 'Mythology and Central Banking', *Kyklos,* 26/2, 1973.

Chapman, Brian, *British Government Observed: Some European Reflections,* George Allen and Unwin, 1963.

Chapman, Brian, *The Profession of Government,* Unwin University Books, 1966.

Chapman, R.J.K., 'Achieving change: inquiries into the public services of Australia and Ireland', *Administration* Vol. 26, No. 4, 1978.

Chubb, Basil, *Cabinet Government in Ireland,* Institute of Public Administration, 1974.

Chubb, Basil, *Government and Politics of Ireland,* Oxford University Press, 1970.

Chubb, B. and Lynch, P., 'An End and a Beginning?' in Chubb and Lynch, eds., *Economic Development and Planning: Readings in Irish Public Administration,* Vol. 1, Institute of Public Administration, 1969.

Clucas, Sir Kenneth, 'Parliament and the Civil Servant' in *Parliament and the Executive,* RIPA, 1982.

Cook, Pat, 'Why we need open Government in Ireland', *Seirbhis Phoibli,* Vol. 6, No. 3, 1985.

Crossman, R., *Inside View,* Cape, 1972.

Deeney, James, *To Cure and To Care,* Glendale Press, 1989.

Devlin Report: Report of Public Services Organisation Review Group 1966-69.

Dell, Edmund, 'Some reflections on cabinet government by a former practitioner', lecture given at London School of Economics and Political Science, 10 May 1979.

Fair, Don, 'The Independence of Central Banks', *The Banker,* 1979.

Fair, Don, 'Relationships between central banks and governments in the determination of monetary policy', SUERF 1980.

Fanning, Ronan, *The Irish Department of Finance 1922-1958,* Institute of Public Administration, 1978.

Farrell, Brian, 'From First Dáil through the Irish Free State' in O'Farrell, B, ed, *De Valera's Constitution and Ours,* Gill and Macmillan, 1988.

Fogarty, Ryan and Lee, *Irish Values and Attitudes,* Dominican Publications, 1984.

Fry, G K, *The Administrative Revolution in Whitehall,* Croom Helm 1981.

Fry, G K, *The Changing Civil Service,* George Allen and Unwin, 1985.

Fulton Committee on the Civil Service 1966-1968, Cmnd 3638.

Gray, A and Jenkins, B, 'Lasting Reforms in Civil Service Management?', *Political Quarterly,* Vol 55, No 4, 1984.

Hardiman, T P, address to Midland Region, IMI, 20 Oct 1982.

Heclo, H., *A Government of Strangers: Executive Politicians in Washington,* Brookings, 1977.

Henderson, Nicholas, *The Private Office,* Weidenfeld and Nicholson, 1984.

Hensey, Brendan, *The Health Services of Ireland,* 4th ed, Institute of Public Administration, 1988.

Humphries, P, *Public Service Employment, An Examination of Strategies in Ireland and other European Countries,* Institute of Public Administration, 1983.

Jackson, P, 'Public Expenditure and Bureaucracy' in Bristow and McDonagh, eds, *Public Expenditure — The Key Issues,* Institute of Public Administration, 1986.

Jackson, P M, *The Political Economy of Bureaucracy,* Philip Allan, 1982.

Johnson, Nevil, 'Who are the policy makers?', *Public Administration,* Vol. 43, autumn 1965.

Kellner, Peter, and Crowther-Hunt, Lord, *The Civil Servants,* MacDonald, 1980.

Kennedy, Kieran, *Irish Banking Review,* March 1982.

Kennedy , K A, Giblin, T, McHugh, D, *The Economic Development of Ireland in the Twentieth Century,* Routledge, 1988.

Kirby, M D, 'Towards the New Federal Administrative Law', *Australian Journal of Public Administration*, Vol. LX, No. 2, 1981.

Kenny, Ivor, *In Good Company*, Gill and Macmillan, 1987.

Lee, Joseph, 'Continuity and Change in Ireland', Thomas Davis Lecture, 11 April 1978.

Lee, Joseph, 'Perspectives on Ireland in the EEC - a Review Essay', *The Economic and Social Review*, 16/1, Oct 1984.

Lee, Joseph, 'A Third Division Team?', *Seirbhis Phoibli*, Vol. 6, No. 1, 1985.

Lee, Joseph, 'Centralisation and Community in Ireland' in Lee, J, ed, *Towards a Sense of Place*, Cork University Press, 1985 (a).

Lee, Joseph, 'Whither Ireland? The Next Twenty-Five Years' in Kennedy, K A, ed, *Ireland in Transition*, RTE/Mercier Press, 1986.

Leemans, A F, 'Recent Trends in the Career Service in European Countries', *International Review of Administrative Sciences*, Vol. 53, 1987.

Lemass, S F, 'The Organisation Behind the Economic Programme', *Administration*, Vol. 9, No 1, 1961.

Lemass, S F, *Leargas*, No 12, Jan/Feb, 1968.

Lynch, Patrick, 'The economist and public policy', *Studies*, Autumn 1953.

McCarthy, R K, *Electoral Policies in Ireland: Party and Parish Pump*, Brandon Books, 1983.

McDowell, Moore, 'A generation of public expenditure growth: Leviathan unchained' in Litton, F, ed, *Unequal Achievement, The Irish Experience 1957-82*, Institute of Public Administration, 1982.

McLellan, D, *Karl Marx: The Legacy*, BBC, 1983.

Mattei, E, ed, *The Mandarins of Western Europe*, John Wiley and Sons, 1975.

Matthews, Alan, 'Economic Consequences of EEC Membership for Ireland' in Coombs, D, ed, *Ireland and the European Communities: Ten Years of Membership*, Gill and Macmillan, 1983.

Mittra, Sid, *Central Bank Versus Treasury: An International Study*, University Press of America, 1979.

Moynihan, Maurice, *Currency and Central Banking in Ireland, 1922-1960*, Central Bank of Ireland, 1975.

Moynihan, Maurice, *Functions of the Department of the Taoiseach*, 2nd ed, Institute of Public Administration, 1960.

Neville-Jones, P, 'The Continental Cabinet System: The Effects of Transposing it to the United Kingdom', *The Political Quarterly*, Vol. 54, No. 3, 1983.

O'Brien of Lothbury, Lord, 'The Independence of Central Banks', address given to Societé Royal d'Economie Publique, 14 Dec 1977.

O Cearbhaill, Tadhg, 'The civil service in its place', *Administration*, Vol 31, No 1, 1982.

O'Doherty, E F, *Administration*, Vol 6, No 2, 1956.

O'Donovan, John, *Studies*, Autumn 1953.

O'Halpin, Eunan, 'Oireachtas Committees: Experience and Prospects' *Seirbhis Phoiblí*, Vol. 7, No 2, 1986.

O Mathúna, Seán, 'The Christian Brothers and the civil service', *Administration*, Vol 3, No. 2, 1956.

Open University Press, *Policies, People and Administration: Block I, The Administrative Context,* 1982.

Peillon, Michael, *Contemporary Irish Society: An Introduction.* Gill and Macmillan, 1982.

Philbin, Most Rev W J, 'Patriotism and the Civil Servant', *Administration,* Vol 8 No 1, 1960.

Policy for Economic Recovery, Fine Gael, Oct 1982.

Pliatzky, L, 'Mandarins, Ministers and the Management of Britain', *the Political Quarterly,* Vol 55, No 1, 1984.

Powell, Enoch, in *Whitehall and Beyond,* BBC Publications, 1964.

Pyne, Peter, 'The Irish Civil Service', *Administration,* Vol. 22 No. 1, 1974.

Raven, J, et al, *Political Culture in Ireland: The Views of Two Generations,* Institute of Public Administration, 1976.

Ridley, F F, ed, *Government and Administration in Western Europe,* Martin Robertson, 1979.

Ridley, F F, 'The British Civil Service and Politics: Principles in Question and Traditions in Flux', *Parliamentary Affairs,* Vol 36, No 1, 1983.

Ridley, F F, 'The Responsibility of Officials in the Democratic Political System' in Leemans, A F and Dunsire, A., eds, *The Public's Servants, Checks on Public Servants in European Countries,* Finn Publishers, 1981.

Roche, R, 'The High Cost of Complaining Irish Style', *Journal of Irish Business and Administrative Research,* 4/2, 1982.

Rodgers, W, *The Politics of Change,* Secker and Warburg, London, 1982.

Rose, Richard, ed, *Policy Marking in Britain,* London 1969.

Rose, Richard, *Changes in Public Employment: A Multi-Dimensional Comparative Analysis,* University of Strathclyde, 1980.

Rose, Richard, 'Public Employment and Public Expenditure', in Bristow and McDonagh, eds, *Public Expenditure — The Key Issues,* Institute of Public Administration, 1986.

Rose and Suleiman, eds, *Presidents and Prime Ministers,* American Enterprise Institute for Public Policy Research, 1982.

Ross, Michael, *Employment in the Public Domain,* ESRI Paper No. 127, 1983.

Smith, Raymond, *Garret: The Enigma. Dr Garret FitzGerald.* Aherlow Publishers, 1985.

Southern, D, in Ridley, F F (ed), *Government and Administration in Western Europe.* Martin Robertson, London, 1979.

Wass, Sir Douglas, 'Government and the Governed', *Listener,* Nov–Dec, 1983.

The Way Forward, The: National Economic Plan 1983-1987, PL 1061.

Whelan, John, 'Open Competition for a Proportion of Senior Civil Service Posts: The Pros and Cons', *Seirbhis Phoiblí,* Vol 4 No 1, 1983.

Whitaker, TK, 'The civil service and development', *Administration,* Vol 9 No 2, 1961.

Weintraub, Robert E, 'Congressional Supervision of Monetary Policy', *Journal of Monetary Economics,* 4, Oct 1978.

Williams, S, in *No Minister: An Inquiry into the Civil Service,* H. Young and A. Slocum, BBC, London.

Wilson, Harold, in *Whitehall and Beyond,* BBC Publications, 1964.

Zijlstra, Dr J, 'Central Banking, a moderate monetarist's view' in *The role of central banks in economic decision making,* Bank of Israel, 1979.